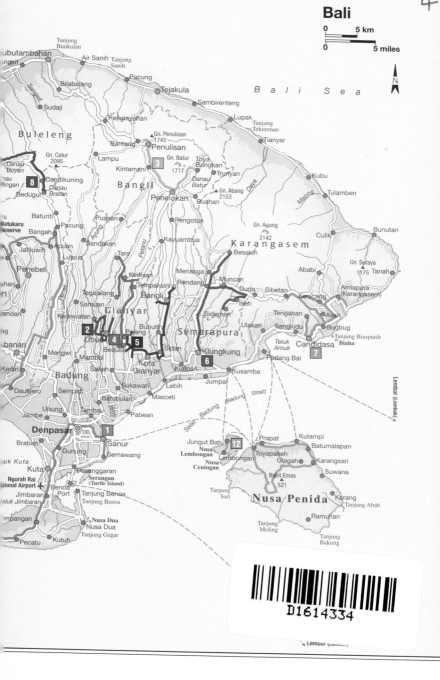

Bali

0   5 km

0   5 miles

N

Bali Sea

INSIGHT GUIDES

BALI

Step by Step

APA PUBLICATIONS **L**
Part of the Langenscheidt Publishing Group

CONTENTS

ABOUT THIS BOOK

Above: Bali sights and attractions.

This *Step by Step Guide* has been produced by the editors of Insight Guides, whose books have set the standard for visual travel guides since 1970. With top-quality photography and authoritative recommendations, this guidebook brings you the very best of Bali in a series of 12 tailor-made tours.

WALKS AND TOURS

The tours in the book provide something to suit all budgets, tastes and trip lengths. As well as covering Bali's many classic attractions, the routes track lesser-known sights and up-and-coming areas. The tours embrace a range of interests, so whether you are an art fan, a gourmet, a lover of flora or have children to entertain, you will find an option to suit.

We recommend that you read the whole of a tour before setting out. This should help you to familiarise yourself with the route and enable you to plan where to stop for refreshments – options for this are shown in the 'Food and Drink' boxes, recognisable by the knife-and-fork sign, on most pages.

On all tours, it's advisable to take a sunhat, suncream and bottled water. For our pick of the walks by theme, consult Recommended Tours For... *(see p.6–7)*.

OVERVIEW

The tours are set in context by this introductory section, giving an overview of Bali to set the scene, plus background information on food and drink, shopping, entertainment, and sports and outdoor activities. A succinct history timeline highlights the key events that have shaped Bali over the centuries.

DIRECTORY

Also supporting the tours is a Directory chapter, comprising a user-friendly, clearly organised A–Z of practical information, our pick of where to stay and select restaurant listings; these eateries complement the more low-key cafés and restaurants that feature within the tours and are intended to offer a wider choice for evening dining. Also included here are some nightlife listings.

The Author

Born and raised in England, Rachel Lovelock's childhood dream was to become a writer and live on a tropical island, but she followed the advice of her careers teacher and worked for a UK-based corporate company instead. She finally realised her dream when she moved to Bali on a whim in 1998. She fell in love with the island and has been living there ever since, writing prolifically for magazines, guidebooks and websites. Her work covers a wide variety of topics, ranging from culture, tourist destinations and activities, to restaurants and luxury villas, embellished with a few personal stories from her heart.

Margin Tips
Shopping tips, historical facts, handy hints and insider information on activities help visitors to make the most of their time in Bali.

Feature Boxes
Notable topics are highlighted in these special boxes.

Key Facts Box
This box gives details of the distance covered on the tour, plus an estimate of how long it should take. It also states where the route starts and finishes, and gives key travel information such as which days are best to do the route or handy transport tips.

Footers
Look here for the tour name, a map reference and the main attraction on the double-page.

Route Map
Detailed cartography shows the tour clearly plotted with numbered dots. For more detailed mapping, see the pull-out map slotted inside the back cover.

Food and Drink
Recommendations of where to stop for refreshment are given in these boxes. The numbers prior to each restaurant/café name link to references in the main text. Restaurants in the Food and Drink boxes are plotted on the maps.

The $ signs at the end of each entry reflect the approximate cost of a two-course meal for one, with a non-alcoholic beverage. These should be seen as a guide only. Price ranges, also quoted on the inside back flap for easy reference, are:

$$$$	over Rp 300,000
$$$	Rp 200,000–300,000
$$	Rp 100,000–200,000
$	below Rp 100,000

ARCHITECTURE

View the ceremonial longhouses of Tenganan (tour 7) the 'Mother Temple' of Besakih (tour 6), the water palace of Taman Ujung (tour 7) and the Brahma Arama Vihara (tour 9).

RECOMMENDED TOURS FOR...

CULTURE SEEKERS

Take your pick from the monuments of Denpasar (tour 1), the museums of Ubud (tour 2), the royal history of Klungkung (tour 6), the temple of Tanah Lot (tour 11) and the fascinating sights of Pejeng and Bangli (tour 5).

FAMILIES WITH KIDS

Swing through the trees like Tarzan at Bali Treetop Adventure Park (tour 8), ride elephants at the Elephant Safari Park (tour 4) and witness glorious culture at Tenganan (tour 7).

FOODIES

Food lovers will relish the restaurants of Seminyak (tour 1) and Ubud (tour 2), while feasting on seafood on the beach at Jimbaran Bay (tour 1) is an experience that all visitors should try.

FLORA AND FAUNA

Bali's beautiful nature is a big draw for visitors; you can observe monkeys and herons (tour 2), elephants (tour 4), dolphins (tour 9) and the magnificent flora of Mt Batukau (tour 11).

SHOPPERS

Test your bartering skills in the markets of Denpasar (tour 1), browse art shops (tour 2), plod the 5km (3-mile) main street of Tegallalang (tour 4) and search for textiles and other cultural treasures in Tenganan (tour 7).

SPORTS ENTHUSIASTS

For diving, snorkelling, surfing and water sports, where better to pursue your passion than Lake Bratan (tour 8), Nusa Lembongan (tour 12), Uluwatu (tour 1) and Medewi (tour 10).

BEACH LOVERS

Sea and sun worshippers will appreciate the white sands of Nusa Lembongan (tour 12), the dark sand bay of Lovina (tour 9) and the simplicity of Pasir Putih (tour 7).

ART BUFFS

Marvel at the artwork in the museums of Ubud (tour 2), a Belgian artist's museum-home in Sanur (tour 1) and the fabulous painted ceilings of the Kerta Gosa at Klungkung (tour 6).

VIEWFINDERS

Be blown away by Batur and Kintamani (tour 3), Bedulu, Tampaksiring and Tegallalang (tour 4), Bangli (tour 5), Pupuan (tour 10) and Jatiluwih and Mt Batukau (tour 11)

OVERVIEW

An overview of Bali's geography, customs and culture, plus illuminating background information on food and drink, shopping, entertainment, sports and outdoor activities and history.

INTRODUCTION

Bali has been described with some of the most hackneyed clichés in travel writing: exotic, seductive, magical. Although these adjectives describe the charms of this island, through overuse they lose their power and pose a dilemma for the writer, since any description less florid seems inadequate.

Above: ready for a purification ceremony at Seseh; Kendongan fish market (near Jimbaran Bay).

Volcanic Island
A chain of six volcanoes, ranging in height between 1,350m (4,400ft) and 3,014m (9,800ft) above sea level, stretches from the west to the east of Bali. The beaches in the south consist of white sand, while beaches in other parts of the island are of dark volcanic sand.

For a tiny island in the world's largest archipelago, Bali has an astonishing diversity. The international airport is located in the southern region of Badung, the urban and commercial centre of Bali. This is where most visitors play and party all day long and late into the night, mostly in the beach towns of Kuta, Legian and Seminyak. The more sedate Sanur and Nusa Dua areas allow for more self-contained hedonism. Yet south Bali is not without redemption, for behind the blatant commercialisation are some of Bali's most traditional aspects. In the regions of Gianyar and Bangli, the contours become softer, the villages smaller and the culture more unfettered. Bali's earliest kingdoms carved out realms in these fertile lands and left behind a legacy of ancient temples. Ubud especially is a magnet for culture, with many of its surrounding villages specialising in particular arts, crafts, dances or musical styles.

Eastward in the regions of Klungkung and Karangasem are areas of striking contrasts, dominated by the island's highest mountain Gunung Agung, the spiritual focus for most

Balinese. Isolated villages, still conservative by nature, continue to maintain artistic traditions and ancient customs. The northern coast of Bali, the region of Buleleng, is mainly agricultural, growing everything from spices to grapes. Mountains almost meet the sea on narrow black sand beaches washed by calm waves.

Western Bali, the region of Jembrana and part of Buleleng, is sometimes dry and sometimes lush, and ignored by most travellers. Sparsely populated yet culturally diverse, a national park with rare wildlife anchors this part of the island. Finally, the southwest Tabanan region is the rice basket of Bali, once home to powerful royal dynasties and today, rural villages scattered on gentle sloping plains watered by crater lakes nestled under hulking volcanoes.

BALI TOURS

Bali has an area of 5,632 sq km (2,175 sq miles), measuring just 90km (55 miles) along the north-south axis and 140km (87 miles) from east to west. The island's compact size means that

most of the country can be explored through scenic drives and walks, very often on day trips.

The 12 tours in this book cover most of the island's main sights, and, with the exception of the Lovina and Singaraja trip (No. 9), are all suitable for visitors based in the south or in Ubud, and designed as single day trips. Visitors who are not restricted to one specific base can, however, link some of the tours and use them as a guide for exploring larger areas of the island – we have suggested possible links in the grey 'Key Facts' boxes at the start of each tour.

With the exception of the Nusa Lembongan route (No. 12), all itineraries are road trips. We recommend that you arrange for a car and driver, so that you can relax and enjoy the scenery – driving in Bali can be dangerous, and road signs can be confusing or inadequate *(see A–Z, p.93)*. Traffic jams are common, especially at rush hour in the built-up areas in the south. Note that Denpasar *(tour 1)*, in particular, is not an easy city to navigate by car due to a complexity of one-way streets and the lack of parking space.

TOURISM

Since the 1960s Bali has been defined and propelled forwards by tourism. Although some anthropologists charge that this has resulted in the loss of Balinese innocence and a commer-cialisation of its traditional culture and values, it is clear that tourism has been the making of Bali over the past few decades. In the island's arts and crafts industry and in the performing arts at least, there can be no doubt of tourism's revitalising effects. Today, thousands of villagers produce craft items both for the local tourism market and for export. Traditional village architects rebuild temples using time-honoured principles, while their university-trained counterparts design luxury hotels incorporating Balinese elements. All of these efforts are part of a creative process that has been going on for centuries in Bali: the resilience of Balinese culture comes from its remarkable ability to adopt, adapt and absorb.

Above from far left: vibrant flowers at Candi Kuning; celebrating an *odilan*, or temple anniversary; Puru Ulun Danu Bratan.

Below: straw boxes for temple offerings.

Language

Balinese people speak Indonesian, but generally revert to Balinese in their homes. English is widely spoken in all the tourist areas, but often not understood in the more remote villages and farming communities. For more information on local languages, *see p.89.* For useful vocabulary, see the inside back cover of this book and also the pull-out map.

CLIMATE

Bali has a tropical climate appropriate to its proximity eight degrees south of the equator. Year-round temperatures average 30°C (86°F). High humidity can be expected during the rainy season between mid-October and mid-April, while humidity is lowest during the dry season, from May to September. The rainy season brings daily downpours, dramatic thunderstorms and overcast days, with the greatest rainfall recorded between December and February. From June to August there is a very refreshing cool breeze, and you can expect constant sunshine. The mountainous regions offer a cooler alternative, especially at night.

Balinese Hindu Culture

Religion is still the central spine of the Balinese way of life and philosophy, with the temple, or *pura,* the focus of every Hindu community on the island. When it is a matter of tradition and spiritual duty, even the young generation swaps its jeans and business suits for a sarong and heads to the temple or to one of the many village events – from a birth celebration, tooth-filing ceremony (to be rid of evil), wedding or cremation. Any visitor who spends more than a few days on the island is certain to witness some kind of temple festival, colourful procession, or ceremony. The *odilan,* or temple anniversary celebration, is a particularly lavish occasion in Bali. As the date varies from one temple to another, you may well have the opportunity to catch one during your visit.

POPULATION

Bali has a population of over 3 million, of which the overwhelming majority is Hindu (noteworthy, given that Indonesia is the world's most populous Muslim nation). There are, however, a few pockets of long-established Muslims, Christians and Buddhists residing in rural areas; people who are usually descendants of enduring populations, with origins elsewhere in the Indonesian-Malaysian region. These people, whose histories in Bali stretch far back, have assimilated to the Balinese identity and are culturally Balinese.

There is also a growing number of Muslim and Christian immigrants from neighbouring islands who come in search of jobs. The new arrivals have settled mainly in the urban areas of southern Bali, where they serve as a cheap labour force. Most people, especially the young, live in the capital city and administrative centre of Denpasar, as well as the tourist areas on the south coast, and the inland town of Ubud.

LOCAL CUSTOMS

There are four types of holiday in Indonesia: religious, national, international and commemorative. Ones that are designated *tanggal merah* (literally red date, or designated in red on a calendar) signify national holidays,

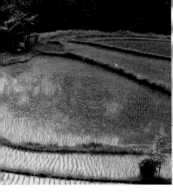

when government offices, schools and banks are closed. However, the majority of shops, restaurants, travel agents and tourist attractions in Bali remain open on these days. Many of the dates of religious holidays vary from year to year.

POLITICS

Bali is one of the 26 provinces of Indonesia, whose president, Susilo Bambang Yudhoyono (SBY), is the chief of state, head of government and supreme commander in chief of the armed forces. After decades under a dictatorship, Indonesia has evolved in the past decade into a democracy. While the country is predominantly Muslim *(see under 'Population', left)*, the government is secular, with a constitutional obligation to protect religious freedom. The Indonesian government officially recognises five religions: Islam, Protestantism, Catholicism, Buddhism and Hinduism.

ECONOMY

In addition to revenue from tourism *(see p.11)*, Bali's economy is sustained by the export of artisanal goods and agricultural products. The chain of mountains dividing the island is responsible for the different climatic conditions and soil types, so Bali produces a huge variety of crops. The southern-central plains are extensively

cultivated – the landscape is dominated by terraced rice fields, but heading inland these become gardens of onions, cabbages and papayas, and in the higher regions coffee, tobacco, cloves, chillies and peanuts, all of which thrive in the cooler climate.

The farmers who live in the rain shadow of the mountain range, in the hot northern-coastal region, cultivate dry-land crops such as maize, cassava, beans and grapes. Fishing and seaweed farming are also important commodities for foreign markets.

It is this contrast of agricultural activities and artistic endeavour, combined with dramatic scenery and a culture long associated with grace and hospitality, that make Bali such an appealing place to visit.

Above from far left: Air Panas, Banjar; rice terraces surrounding Sideman village; outrigger boats at Amed.

Below: Buddha image at Brahma Arama Vihara.

FOOD AND DRINK

The island caters for every taste, from street-food served out of boxes balanced on bicycles and prepared at the road side, to gourmet cuisine presented in world-class restaurants.

The exciting news for epicures is that both local and international restaurants can be found in abundance in Bali's tourist areas, while the range of styles, settings, ambiences and cuisines on offer is huge. The mouth-watering creations of Bali's five-star chefs are testament to the quality and diversity of the fresh produce of this fertile island; by creating a demand for premium fruit and vegetables (including organic produce), suppliers, retailers, restaurateurs and hoteliers are not only supporting the local farmers, but showcasing Bali's bountiful harvest.

Below: beware those fiery chillies.

LOCAL CUISINE

Indonesian Cuisine

Indonesian cuisine varies greatly by region. Many speciality dishes were influenced by the early Arabic, Chinese, Indian and Dutch traders and settlers. Flavoursome local curries incorporate freshly ground spices and seasonings such as lemongrass, ginger, kaffir lime leaves and tamarind. Simple Indonesian dishes include *nasi campur*, comprised of rice and a selection of vegetables, meat or fish, egg and other accompaniments; *nasi goreng* (fried rice); *mie goreng* (fried noodles); *sate* served with a sweet and spicy peanut sauce; *cap cay*, consisting of wok-tossed seasonal vegetables; and *gado-gado*, a warm salad of blanched, mixed vegetables, tofu and hard-boiled egg served with peanut sauce.

Staple Balinese Fare

In everyday Balinese cooking, prepared by the women of the island and eaten

at home as well as at *warungs* (small road-side stalls), the staple ingredient is rice, eaten with small portions of spicy vegetables, fish, meat and eggs, and accompanied by *sambal* (hot paste ground from fiery chillies). This type of dish, again known as *nasi campur*, is usually cooked in the early morning and consumed whenever hunger hits. Another very popular way of cooking is to wrap minced and highly seasoned meat, fish or poultry in banana-leaf parcels and steam them, or set the parcels directly onto hot coals to roast. Known as *tum*, these banana-leaf packets are served in most Balinese homes. *Pepes ikan*, where minced spiced fish is the filling, is a favourite delicacy: the banana leaf seals in the juices, and biting into the parcel produces a moist, fragrant, smoky explosion in the mouth.

Balinese cooking favours the use of coconuts (either grated or as coconut milk), peanuts (which are ground into a paste to form a sweet and spicy sauce), and salted and fermented shrimp paste, used to enliven and add depth to dishes. *Tempe*, a nutty slab made from fermented soy beans, is a delicious and inexpensive source of protein. Fresh spices, garlic, onions and hot fresh chillies are also used in abundance, meaning that dishes – while deliciously fragrant – can also be tantalisingly hot.

Balinese – and Indonesian – desserts include *bubuh injin*, which is a sweet and sticky black rice pudding, named after the colour of the rice husk and served with coconut milk sauce. *Pisang goreng* is banana fried in batter and served with syrup, while *kue dadar* are little crêpe parcels filled with palm sugar, vanilla and grated coconut. Other favourites include sweets, jellies, tapioca and sticky cakes, which are generally garnished with grated coconut and presented in shades of pink and green.

Festive Dishes

In contrast to everyday dishes, which are prepared by the women of the island, special ceremonial food is prepared in an elaborate manner by the men, and then eaten communally. The dishes, which can be ordered in advance at some restaurants, include *babi guling* (a slow-cooked spit-roasted pig stuffed with onion, garlic, peppercorns and herbs, and brushed with crushed turmeric), *bebek betutu* (duck stuffed with spices, wrapped in banana leaves and smoked overnight in an earth-oven), *lawar* (spicy raw meat mashed with grated coconut and blood) and *sate lilit* (satay of spiced, minced meat or fish with an infusion of coconut, pressed onto a lemongrass skewer).

WHERE TO EAT

In Seminyak, Kuta, Sanur, Ubud and Nusa Dua and the surrounding areas, there are restaurants serving upmarket international cuisine from Italy, Greece, France, Spain, Mexico, India, Morocco, China, Japan, Korea, Thailand and

Above from far left: preparing *babi guling* at Gianyar market; road-side fruit for sale.

Imported Alcohol

While imported spirits and fine wines from around the world are available in Bali, the selection is often limited and prices are excessive due to the application of high customs and excise tax. This is causing great concern to Bali's business people, as it has the potential to damage the island's hospitality industry.

more, as well as local specialities from Bali and across the Indonesian archipelago. Simple speciality restaurants from Sumatra, Java, Sulawesi and other Indonesian islands are also to be found mainly in the south of Bali, in particular in Denpasar and parts of Kuta and Seminyak. Outside of the tourist areas you will find small *warungs* (eateries) serving simple Indonesian dishes.

For the visitor, genuine Balinese cuisine (as opposed to Indonesian or Indonesian-Chinese food) can be difficult to find. But if you search hard enough, you can track down truly local dishes at some market stalls (especially on main market days), at some *warung* and at the handful of restaurants now aware that visitors actually want to try authentic Balinese cuisine.

Some restaurants specialise in serving food by type, such as seafood, comfort food, vegetarian food or fusion food. Five-star resorts typically have superb restaurants and world-class chefs. Many restaurants also have their own bakeries on the premises, serving delicious breads, pastries and cakes.

Seminyak

Seminyak's fashionable 'Eat Street' stretches from Jl Laksmana and Jl Kayu Ayu to Jl Petitenget, and if you were to eat out there every night, it would take over a month to appraise every restaurant on this strip. There is something to suit all budgets here, and competition means that standards remain high.

As you walk through the doors of some of these restaurants, you may be excused for believing that you have been transported to anywhere else but Bali – from a Greek island, to a Moroccan kasbah, to a Japanese izakaya. A number of restaurants offer alfresco dining in fabulous locations overlooking the Indian Ocean, while others have dazzling rice-field views – in fact some have even extended into the rice fields.

Others still, although situated on busy streets, invite you to escape from the sound of traffic, the elements and perhaps the buzz and atmosphere of Bali, to a truly exceptional experience, all in comfort and without distractions to blight your pleasure. Expect super-chic decor and constantly evolving, sophisticated menus.

LOCAL DRINKS

Beer

As for thirst quenchers, the bestselling brand of beer in Bali is Bintang, produced by Multi Bintang Indonesia, an Indonesian subsidiary of Heineken. This 5 percent pilsner (clear, bottom-fermented lager beer) is delightfully refreshing when served ice-cold. It is readily available almost everywhere, from bars and restaurants to supermarkets and convenience stores, but may be a little harder to find outside of the tourist areas or in Muslim-owned stores and eateries, and may be served warm in the villages.

Tuak, Arak and Brem

Other local brews include *tuak* (palm-beer, strange-tasting and intoxicating), and *arak,* the local firewater, made from palm sap and drunk either neat or with a sweet mixer. Two popular drinks enjoyed by tourists are Arak Attack (*arak* and orange juice) and Arak Madu (*arak*, water, honey, with a slice of lime). Be warned, however, that *arak* has an unrefined character and has been known to cause deaths due to tainting with methanol. Brem Bali, a sweet rice wine, is another popular, traditional drink, made from glutinous, sticky white rice known as *ketan,* together with a smaller amount of *injin,* Indonesian black rice. Besides being a beverage, it is a requirement for many Hindu ceremonies.

Balinese Wine

Surprisingly, grapes have been cultivated in the hot and arid northern coastal region of the island since the beginning of the 20th century. It was only a few decades ago, however, after multiple trials and errors impeded by parasites and other vine diseases that grapes were grown satisfactorily on a large scale and marketed all over the Indonesian archipelago. This led to the creation of an industry that is not traditionally associated with Bali, and 1994 saw the establishment of Hatten Wines. The company now produces a total of eight different all-Balinese wines, which are natural and free of colouring, flavouring and concentrates.

Fresh Fruit Juices

Bali is famous for its fresh fruit and vegetable juices, including pineapple, avocado laced with chocolate, or innovative blends such as passionfruit, watermelon and papaya. Meanwhile, the fresh young coconut drink known as *kelapa muda* is either sipped straight from the shell or served with ice and supplemented by slithers of slippery young coconut flesh.

Above from far left: beautifully presented sushi at Ku De Ta (*see p.103*); Italian trattoria-style restaurant in Seminyak; lobster dumplings.

Indonesian Rijsttafel

Rijsttafel, literally meaning 'rice-table' and originating from the Dutch plantation owners, is a great way to selectively sample the Indonesian cuisine. It is easy to find, presented as a buffet at most of the middle-market and upmarket tourist hotels as well as at restaurants that cater for large numbers. This elaborate meal includes an assortment of meat, seafood and vegetable dishes, salads and spring rolls, including *sate*, accompanied by rice crackers and a collection of pickles, spicy *sambals* and sauces, and followed by local desserts and fresh fruits. The objective is to feature not only an array of multi-textured specialities, but also flavours, colours and degrees of spiciness. The Balinese version is called *megibung* and will combine local delicacies with Balinese *bumbu* – a spice paste that varies from village to village. The spicy *sambals* are optional condiments in consideration of personal palates.

SHOPPING

From modern malls to hinterland villages where traditional craftsmen sell their wares to the art galleries of Ubud and the silver emporia of Celuk, Bali has something to suit all shoppers' tastes.

Opening Times
Shopping malls are generally open daily from 10am until 10 or 11pm, while the shops in Kuta and Seminyak are open from 9am until 9pm. Smaller shops and wholesale outlets (such as the shops in Tegallalang) will close at 5pm and are closed on Sundays.

The Balinese are renowned for their artistic skills, and you will find lots of souvenirs to take back home. As the range of local crafts, art, antiques, jewellery and clothes is so huge, it takes a bit of hunting and rummaging to find what's right for you.

KUTA

Jl Legian and Kuta Square present a hotchpotch of trendy branded outlets, souvenir shops and fashion boutiques, together with surfwear concept stores stocking everything you could possibly need associated with surfing and the attendant lifestyle.

Discovery Mall

For a shopping mall excursion, you might want to visit the beachfront 'Discovery Mall', the biggest and the most complete one-stop shopping mall ever built in Bali. Fully air-conditioned, the three-floor mall attracts plenty of custom with two department stores, global lifestyle branded boutiques, local retailers, a food court, beach-side cafés and more.

KEROBOKAN AND SEMINYAK

In Kerobokan, you can choose to rummage for treasures through clut-

Right: clothing to keep cool in.

tered little stores crammed with curios and antiques, browse classy homeware shops or wander through huge warehouses displaying their ranges of high-quality furniture.

In trendy Seminyak you will find a whole host of designer boutiques. Tropical panache collections feature ethnic chic designs executed in richly garnished silks, diaphanous chiffons and strong, deep colours, perfect for Bali's glamorous night scene.

UBUD

If you are looking to purchase paintings, Ubud is the place to conduct your search. Classic, contemporary and abstract artworks, fine art, folk art and decorative wall panels, can all be found in the town's numerous galleries and art shops.

Denpasar

Unadventurous consumers will not be attracted by the prospect of a shopping trip to Denpasar. However, if you are a bold and brave bargainhunter, a spree within the heart of Bali's bustling provincial capital will probably prove to be the most rewarding experience of all. Visit Denpasar's vibrant markets, where everything and anything, including handicrafts and artwork, is available somewhere amid the chaos of the heaped stalls lining the narrow, crowded alleyways.

BALI'S HINTERLAND

Intrepid shoppers may also wish to visit the stone- and woodcarving villages in Bali's hinterland. Batubulan is renowned for its stone carvings, which are exhibited all along the main road, while the village of Mas is famous for woodcarving, its thoroughfare solidly lined with craft shops where you can watch the carvers at work.

TEGALLALANG

Alternatively, you could plod the 5km (3-mile) main street of Tegallalang, where you will find candles, mirrors, painted balsa-wood cats, flowers and frogs, batik lampshades, wrought-iron picture frames, banana-leaf boxes, dreamcatchers and bamboo windchimes galore, at half the price you would pay in Kuta.

CELUK

Finally, visit the silver emporiums of Celuk, strung along 3km (2 miles) of main road flanked by a maze of backstreets chock-a-block with workshops and smaller outlets. Here, ornate silver rings, bangles, necklaces, bracelets, pendants and accessories, set with precious and semi-precious stones, are produced by master craftsmen whose sterling skills and trade secrets have been passed down through generations of families.

Above from far left: batik scarves, and kites, for sale in Pasar Ubud.

Bartering
In markets, small shops and at street stalls, you are expected to haggle for your purchases where no price is indicated. Don't ask for an overly low price, as this will insult the vendor; ask instead how much the item costs, then whether this is the best price they can offer. Wait for the retailer to respond and never mention the amount of money you are prepared to pay. Tell them that this is more than you wanted to spend and ask if they could let you have the item for less. Continue this process for as long as the vendor offers a lower price. When they won't go any lower, thank them and head for the door. If they let you leave, that really was the best offer. Wait 15 minutes, go back, say you have reconsidered and will accept the last price.

ENTERTAINMENT

Bali is well known for its cultural entertainment. Theatre, dance, music and drama play a very important role in Balinese life, which in turn spills over into the island's many festivals.

Hindu ceremonies in Bali inevitably involve music and dance, which are performed as offerings designed to please the gods who are attending the ceremony, while also being enthusiastically enjoyed by the villagers. With the advent of tourism, the performing arts took on a new role in Bali. Dance troupes and music ensembles now have much more opportunity to be active, and are able to earn a living by performing at hotels and restaurants. Few places in the world can claim such a rich and varied environment of performing arts. This creative energy is also being harnessed in a bid to bring foreign creative talent to the island through festivals.

Negara Bull Races

Said to have originated as a simple ploughing competition, this extraordinary contest, which takes place on Sunday mornings from July through to October, features Bali's sleekest, most handsome water buffaloes. Each race involves two pairs of bulls running against each other around a 2km (1¼-mile) track. Each pair is hitched to a gaily painted wooden chariot driven by a precariously balanced, whip-happy jockey. Festooned with strings of bells, silks and decorative harness, every winning team gains a point for its club, with the most stylish contenders picking up bonus points for the splendour of their presentation.

Dance

Balinese cultural performances are visual, entertaining and exciting, and can be appreciated by adults and children of all ages. There are numerous dance troupes on the island, and many different Balinese dance dramas exist, most of which have evolved from sacred rituals. The dances are often typified by subtle, controlled gestures and a fixed mask-like face with unfocused eyes and closed lips. The dancer's limbs form precise angles and the head sinks down so far that the neck disappears. At other times, gestures replicate nature, hands flutter like a bird in flight, and limbs follow sudden changes of direction as the performers move in slow, horizontal zigzagging

circles. The eyes become expressive and beguiling as they flicker and dance, movements become jerky, sometimes provocative and occasionally erotic. Performances take place daily at tourist centres and are an integral part of almost every temple festival, accompanied by the shimmering, jangling, clashing, syncopated sounds of traditional Balinese gamelan music. Many of the island's large hotels meanwhile host cultural evenings two or three times a week.

FESTIVALS

Bali Arts Festival

The Bali Arts Festival is an annual fiesta of Balinese and Indonesian artistic traditions and culture. It lasts a full month and is held at Bali Arts Centre, Taman Budaya, in Denpasar. The festival showcases daily cultural performances, dance dramas, theatre, traditional and modern music, historical exhibitions, classical palace dances, handicraft exhibitions, garment and jewellery exhibitions, puppet shows, competitions and other related cultural commercial activities, presented by every region in Bali and beyond. The festival opens in June.

Bali Kite Festival

The Bali Kite Festival is held every year in July, when the winds are strong. It takes place at Padanggalak, Sanur, and is actually a seasonal religious fes-

tival intended to send a message to the gods for abundant crops and harvests. Traditional giant kites, measuring up to 4 by 10m (13 by 33ft) in size, are made and flown competitively by teams from different villages.

Ubud Writers and Readers Festival

The annual Ubud Writers and Readers Festival generally takes place in October. Lasting a few days, it comprises an action-packed programme of workshops, readings, keynote presentations, panel discussions, interviews, book launches, dance performances, poetry slams and lively literary lunches. The well-attended, highly regarded festival attracts literary artists, writers, readers, participants and observers from all over the world.

Nusa Dua Festival

Usually held in October, the Nusa Dua Festival is a gala week of special events designed to engage the imagination of both the casual visitor and long-time lovers of Bali. The festival is officially opened with a grand parade before presenting some of Bali's finest performing arts, as well as traditional dance, music and drama performances from other provinces across the Indonesian archipelago. Handicraft exhibitions and displays are also showcased. This festival has been a regular event since 1997 and is based on a theme that changes every year.

Above from far left: *legong* dance performance at Ubud Municipal Hall; giant dragon kite.

Nyepi

If you are visiting Bali in March or April you may be there for Nyepi, or Balinese New Year, which occurs on the day following the dark moon of the spring equinox. This is when the island retreats into silence for 24 hours. On this darkest of nights the Balinese will not cook, work or travel, there are no flights into or out of Bali, shops remain closed, all streets are deserted and no lights are switched on. On the night before Nyepi, exciting street carnival processions take place as the evil spirits are driven away with huge, scary, highly creative papier-mâché monsters known as *Ogoh Ogoh*. Hotels are exempt from Nyepi's rigorous practices, but the streets and beaches outside will be closed to both pedestrians and vehicles.

SPORTS AND OUTDOOR ACTIVITIES

Outdoor activities for all ages, from water sports to golf, horse riding and birdwatching, are plentiful in Bali. A number of specialist adventure tour companies take the adrenalin up a notch with a range of exciting excursions.

Above: boards for hire and snorkelling.

Bali presents a wealth of outdoor activities, not to mention adventure sports such as river rafting, mountain cycling, jungle trekking and four-wheel-drive expeditions. Most companies provide a door-to-door pick-up and drop-off service, and just about every attraction on the island is child-friendly.

WATER SPORTS

Diving and Snorkelling

Bali is the ideal location for learning to dive or diving for pleasure among some of the world's finest tropical reefs. The water is warm, and the marine life is abundant. Reputable dive schools, dive resorts and operators offer facilities, equipment and tuition for every PADI course, from beginners' discovery dives to the highest recreational level (*see p.77*).

Surfing

Bali is renowned as one of the great surfing meccas of the world, offering more than 20 top-quality breaks. The peak surf season is April through October, when the southeast trade winds blow offshore and the full force of the solid southern ocean swells hit the reefs around Kuta, Nusa Dua and the Bukit Peninsula. These are a great draw for veteran surfers, and the breaks found at Padang Padang and Uluwatu (*see p.28*), with its famous entry cave, are world-class barrelling reefbreaks. Meanwhile, for novices and surfers of intermediate ability, there are plenty of mellow beachbreaks.

Other Water Sports

Other water sports, such as windsurfing and water-skiing, are all easy to arrange in Bali. Hotels and tourist agencies/information offices should have details.

OTHER ACTIVITIES

Fishing, eco-tours, bungy-jumping and four-wheel-drive or bike tours are among the activities on offer in Bali. The following may also appeal:

Bird Watching

The inland forests around Bedugul (*see p.61*) and Mt Batukau (*see p.73*) are abundant with birdlife. Of particular

note are jewel-coloured kingfishers, a common sight along the island's many river banks.

Golf

Bali's five spectacular golf courses are all open to non-members and set in mountain, cliff-top and beach-side locations. The Handara Kosaido Country Club in Bedugul (see p.61) is located in the caldera of an ancient volcano and considered to be one of the most beautiful golf courses in the world.

Horse Riding

There are several stables and equestrian resorts on the island offering riding adventures through rice fields, villages, monsoon forest, and along the beach. Most stables provide a good selection of well-trained horses with varying temperaments, energies and sizes to suit all ages and levels of experience.

Mountain Cycling

Specialist adventure tour companies offer exciting mountain cycling tours, which also give an insight into the traditional Balinese lifestyle. Starting at around 1,100m (3,575ft) above sea level, each tour is an exhilarating descent through farms, hamlets and lush valleys, past ancient temples and beautiful rice fields. Each has a number of stops built in, allowing participants to sample some of the indigenous tropical fruits and spices and absorb the beauty of the region.

Paragliding

A number of paragliding clubs operate from the Bukit Peninsula, taking off from the cliff top some 80m (262ft) above Timbis beach, on the southernmost tip of the island. Harnessed to these non-motorised inflatable wings, it is possible to soar over everything from coral reefs to Hindu temples, and the views of the ridgeline are spectacular. Experience is not necessary, as tandem flights for all ages can be arranged with professional instructors and the latest equipment. The on-shore trade winds blow consistently from the southeast from June through September, making this ridge flyable on most days.

Trekking

The diversity of the island allows visitors anything from gentle hikes through rice fields, jungle, rainforests and national parks to challenging mountain treks in the dry season (see p.42).

White-Water Rafting

White-water rafting is an action-packed journey through class II and III rapids, against an awesome backdrop of rainforest, gorges, rice terraces and dramatic waterfalls on the Ayung, Telaga Waja and Unda rivers. There are quite a number of different operators, the most reputable of which maintain exemplary safety standards with highly trained and experienced guides piloting the safety-equipped rafts. Hot showers at the end are followed by a buffet feast.

Above from far left: surfing at Dream Beach, Nusa Lembongan; Beach football; ready to hit the waves.

HISTORY: KEY DATES

Bali's strategic geographical location made it an important stopping point on the maritime trade route, which in turn brought about Dutch colonisation. Today, though, tourism is the island's biggest industry.

EARLY PERIOD AND MIDDLE AGES

2500– 1500BC	Migrants from southern China and mainland Southeast Asia reach the archipelago and mix with aboriginal peoples.
300	Bronze-age culture in Bali.
AD78	Indian civilisation begins to make an impact.
500	Chinese traders mention the Buddhist kingdom of P'oli (Bali).
800	Buddhist Warmadewa dynasty rules Bali.
1000	Airlangga becomes king in East Java and his brother, Anak Wungsu, rules Bali (1035); Javanese influence increases in Bali; during civil war in Java, Bali becomes independent (1045).
1200	Javanese Singasari kingdom retakes Bali (1284); Kublai Khan attacks Java, and Bali breaks free again (1292).
1300	Javanese Majapahit kingdom conquers Bali (1343); Gelgel kingdom unifies Bali (1383).

MAJAPAHIT GOLDEN AGE

1400	Islam spreads to the archipelago and Majapahit begins to disintegrate; Bali becomes a haven for Hindu-Buddhists from Java.
1500	Golden Age for Bali under King Waturenggong; first Dutch arrive in Bali (1597).
1600	Dutch East India Company sets up a trading post in Batavia (Jakarta), West Java; civil war breaks out in Bali (1651); rebellion ends, and Klungkung (Semarapura) is founded (1681).
1700	Bali fractures into rival kingdoms, leading to continuous warfare; Bali controls East Java and Lombok.

EUROPEAN INFLUENCE

1839	Danish trader Mads Lange opens a trading port at Kuta.
1849	North Bali is conquered through Dutch military force.

Bali Bomb Memorial
The 2002 bombing is commemorated with a carved stone monument in Kuta, close to the site of the attack. It is set with a large marble plaque bearing the names and nationalities of those who died, flanked by the national flags of the victims' countries.

1894–6	Karangasem dynasty in Lombok and East Bali falls to the Dutch.
1898	The Dutch take control of Gianyar.
1900	The Dutch defeat royal families of Badung and Tabanan (1906), and Klungkung (1908).
1917	Devastating earthquake hits Bali.
1920–39	New artistic developments during the 1920s and 1930s.

Above from far left: Dewa Agung arriving in Gianyar to nego- tiate with the Dutch, 1906; artwork (1957) by I Nyoman Madia in Ubud's Museum Puri Lukisan.

WORLD WAR II AND INDONESIAN INDEPENDENCE

| 1942–5 | Japanese Occupation during World War II; declaration of Republic of Indonesia on 17 August 1945, after Japanese surrender. |
| 1945–9 | Dutch create State of Eastern Indonesia that includes Bali; after war of independence, the UN recognises Indonesia, and Bali becomes a province. |

POST-INDONESIAN INDEPENDENCE

1963	Mt Gunung Agung erupts, causing thousands of deaths and destroying many temples and villages.
1966	Suharto replaces Sukarno as president of Indonesia.
1986	Nusa Dua is developed into a high-class tourist resort area.
1998	Asian economic crisis hits Indonesia; riots in Jakarta leave over 500 dead. President Suharto resigns amid violent demonstrations.
1999	Rioting when Megawati Sukarnoputri, favoured candidate for president, is not selected; the situation returns to normal when she becomes vice-president. Visitors and residents of other islands seek refuge on Bali when regional conflicts erupt.
2001	Megawati replaces President Abdurrahman Wahid, who resigns over corruption charges.
2002	Terrorist bombs in Kuta kill more than 200 people, mostly foreign tourists. Visitors stay away; many Balinese lose jobs.
2003	SARS outbreak and war in Iraq reduce visitor numbers.
2004	President Megawati loses re-election bid to Susilo Bambang Yudhoyono, after heavily contested polls run twice.
2005	On 1 October, three terrorist suicide bombs explode, one in Kuta Square and two on Jimbaran Beach. Twenty people are killed.
2009	A record year, with 2,229,945 foreign visitors to Bali.
2010	Last at-large suspect in 2002 Bali bombings killed in Jakarta raid.

WALKS AND TOURS

SANUR, DENPASAR AND ULUWATU

Drop by an expatriate artist's beach-front home, visit the museums and markets of Bali's capital city, mingle with monkeys, watch the sunset from a cliff-top perch and finish with a seaside seafood feast.

DISTANCE 80km (50 miles)
TIME A full day
START Sanur
END Jimbaran Bay
POINTS TO NOTE

This busy full-day tour is a good one for those staying in the south (ie Kuta, Seminyak, Sanur, Jimbaran or Nusa Dua). Hire a car and driver for the day; the driver will wait for you whenever you want to stop. Note that the centre of Denpasar involves some walking. Note, too, that the markets and streets of the city are not for the faint-hearted and can be rather daunting if you are new to Bali; the Denpasar city element can, however, simply be excluded from the tour if preferred. Visitors interested in horticulture should follow this route on either a Tuesday or a Friday, when the Bali Hyatt in Sanur conducts tours of its gardens at 10am. If you opt for sunset at the surfer hang-outs at Uluwatu, note there are a lot of steep steps there.

This tour takes you from the historic village of Sanur to the markets and sights of the island's bustling capital, before heading down to a dramatic cliff-top temple and the surfing scene at Uluwatu, on Bali's southwest tip.

SANUR

The prosperous village of **Sanur ❶** is synonymous with gracious living, vine-draped coral walls, majestic trees and a 5km (3-mile) golden sandy shoreline within a gentle reef-sheltered lagoon, offering safe swimming, wakeboarding and windsurfing. A paved esplanade that runs the length of the beach was recently saved from erosion by an impressive landscaping and conservation project that has also safeguarded the coral reef. Sanur was Bali's original tourist enclave, with the island's first simple guest rooms in the 1940s heralding the age of modern tourism. Today, the beach front is laced with a string of medium-range and luxury hotels, and the access roads are lined with numerous art and craft shops.

Bali Hyatt Gardens

Start with breakfast beside the beach at the **Bali Hyatt** ❷ (Jl Danau Tamblingan 89, Sanur; tel: 0361-281234; www.bali.resort.hyatt.com), after which you can stroll around the hotel's famous gardens, created by Australian landscape designer Made Wijaya – maybe participating in a guided tour (Tue and Fri 10am; free). An impressive series of terraces descends to a water garden and several other exquisite botanical and themed gardens, including a tropical white one inspired by Sissinghurst in England.

Museum Le Mayeur

Next stop is the **Museum Le Mayeur** ❸ (Jalan Hang Tuah, Pantai Sanur; tel: 0361-286164; Tue–Sun 8am–2pm; charge), located on Sanur beach north of the Grand Bali Beach Hotel.

The Belgian (Brussels) painter Adrien-Jean Le Mayeur de Merpres (1880–1958) lived in Bali from 1932 until shortly before his death in 1958.

Above from far left: the beach at Sanur; Museum Le Mayeur.

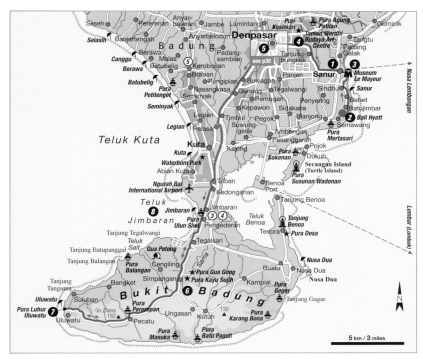

Above: temple deity and Padmasana shrine at Pura Jagatnatha, Denpasar.

Sometimes described as Indonesia's answer to Gauguin, Le Mayeur married the *legong* dancer *(see tour 2, p.41)*, Ni Polok, a beauty who was only 16 when they met; he was 53. His only model, she appears numerous times, always bare-breasted, in his colourful Impressionistic paintings. Before his death, Le Mayeur donated to the government his studio-house with its few remaining works; it was then turned into a museum managed by Ni Polok until her death in 1986. The brackish sea air has unfortunately taken its corrosive toll on the paintings, but the house retains a lingering air of nostalgia and romance.

Arts Around Town

From Sanur, take the main Denpasar road west for 6km (3¾ miles) and drop by the **Taman Werdhi Budaya Art Centre ④** (Jl Nusa Indah; tel: 0361-222776; Tue–Sun 8am–5pm; charge), home to an impressive collection of traditional and modern Balinese art, including Barong and Rangda dance

costumes. From mid-June to July, the annual Bali Arts Festival takes place here, with daily performances, along with displays of arts and crafts from Bali and the Indonesian archipelago.

DENPASAR

Now head 2km (1¼ miles) further west into the city of **Denpasar ⑤**, Bali's provincial capital. Originally known as Badung, the city is a growing metropolis characterised by winding alleyways, traffic jams, confusing signs, and illogical-seeming one-way streets. Many immigrants have settled here, including Chinese, Arab and Indian merchants. However, the old provincial kingdoms and villages of this densely populated area still function in very much the traditional way in terms of religious practice and local community government.

Museum Bali

Off Jalan Surapati, take a left turn to the **Museum Bali ④** (Jl Let. Kol Wisnu; tel: 0361-222680; Sat–Thur 8am–4pm, Fri 8.30am–1pm; charge), established in 1932 by German artist Walter Spies (1895–1942) for the preservation of traditional Balinese arts and crafts. The displays, in several pavilions from different parts of the island, include archaeological finds, dance masks, textiles, paintings and architectural illustrations of the Balinese temples, providing an unrivalled exhibition.

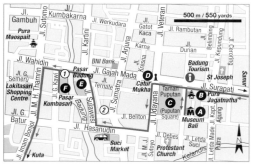

Pura Jagatnatha

Next door to the museum is **Pura Jag-atnatha B**, a territorial temple built in 1953 and dedicated to Sanghyang Widhi Wasa, lord of the universe. Although the temple is open during daylight hours, you will probably not be allowed in (there isn't much to see); but just peer through the gate at the towering white stone *padmasana* (lotus throne) topped by the gilded relief image of Sanghyang Widhi Wasa. The temple, which is popular among local people, embodies the importance given to monotheism, as promoted by the Indonesian government.

Puputan Square

Across the street is **Puputan Square C**, commemorating a suicidal battle of the Rajas of Badung against the Dutch Militia in 1906 and with a bronze memorial to those who lost their lives at its centre. At the square's northwest corner is the main intersection that leads to Veteran Street and all the major streets of Gajah Mada, with their rows of Chinese shops. In the middle of the intersection is the great **Catur Muka D** statue, representing Batara Guru, lord of the four directions. Four different Hindu gods face different directions: Mahadeva (west), Vishnu (north), Ishvara (east) and Brahma (south).

Streets of Textiles and Gold

You are now in the heart of Denpasar; not many visitors come this far into the city, but those who are prepared to brave the crowded streets and busy traffic will discover some unique shopping experiences. Not many people here speak English, but don't let that put you off: take time to enjoy the sights, sounds and aromas of this vibrant, historical city.

Walk 1km (½ mile) south down Jl Udayana and turn right into **Jl Hasa-nudin**, where Bali's gold (18–24 carat) shops are clustered. These shops are all very similar, but the Balinese designs are attractive, and the prices are much lower than in the West.

From here, cross the road north into **Jl Sulawesi**, Denpasar's fabric street, devoted to textiles of all descriptions. Shake off the commission hunters who will try to latch on to you, offering to be your guide, and make your own way to Jl Gajah Mada at the northern end of Jl Sulawesi. Turn left and pause at **Hong-kong**, see ①, for lunch; this extremely popular Chinese restaurant is frequented by expatriates as well as locals.

Food and Drink 🍴

① HONGKONG
Jl Gajah Mada 99, Denpasar; tel: 0361-434845; daily 10am–10pm; $$
This respected Chinese restaurant has a faded grandeur, with fluted pillars and gaudy decor. Service is fast and the menu extensive, offering delicacies such as scallops, sea cucumber with Chinese mushrooms, crispy pigeon, frogs' legs, and banana *à la Sichuan*.

Seafood Feast
The Jimbaran seafood feast is synonymous with holidays in Bali. Beaches are typically lined with cafés serving that day's fishy catch. As you watch the sun set over the sea, barbecued fish, giant prawns, lobster, squid and clams, accompanied by rice, the tasty Balinese water spinach known as *kangkung*, and delicious home-made Balinese sauces, will be brought to your table.

An alternative lunch option is **Rumah Makan Betty**, see ⑪②, a simple little eating house in Jl Sumatra, the road parallel and east of Jl Sulawesi. This is the place to escape from the heat and chaos of the street and relax with a cool drink and a Javanese speciality.

Marketplaces
Immediately to the west of Jl Sulawesi are the two biggest marketplaces in Bali, the chaotic **Pasar Badung** ❺ and **Pasar Kumbasari** ❻, positioned along opposite banks of the polluted Tukad Badung River. Pasar Badung is where the local people do their shopping, with each of the market's three floors dedicated to different products – ranging from fresh produce and flower petal offerings on the ground floor to dried foodstuffs and cooking utensils on the middle floor. The top floor specialises in items such as temple parasols, brass bells, baskets and garden tools. Pasar Kumbasari is another rabbit warren, with small shops specialising mainly in handicrafts, souvenirs and artworks.

THE BUKIT

Head back to the main road and travel south 55km (34 miles), skirting the resort areas of **Kuta** and **Seminyak** *(see box opposite)*, past Jimbaran where we return for dinner *(see p.34)*, all the way to the **Bukit Peninsula** ❻ and Pura Luhur Uluwatu.

Bali's lemon-shaped, southernmost peninsula is an arid limestone tableland that stands out in sharp contrast to the island's lush, alluvial plains. Its dramatic coastline is pounded by a challenging surf that has made it a surfing mecca.

In the 1970s, Nusa Dua, on the southeast coast of the Bukit, was chosen as the location for the most ambitious resort project in Indonesia's history, resulting in a tourist enclave of wide paved lanes and manicured gardens, white-sand beaches, restaurants, a shopping mall, a conference centre and a golf course to support the five-star resorts.

It wasn't until much later, however, that the infrastructure of the rest of the peninsula improved sufficiently to support the development of its remote and magnificent cliff-edge sites. Since 2000, the Bukit has become the most upmarket destination on the island, with some of Bali's most opulent villas, glamorous private estates and boutique hotels.

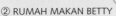

Food and Drink ⑪
② RUMAH MAKAN BETTY
Jl Sumatra 56, Denpasar, tel: 0361-224502; daily 9am–9pm; $
This long-established eatery with plain walls, simple furnishings and views over a busy street serves bargain Chinese and Javanese specialities including *sayur lodeh* vegetable soup with coconut milk, and *cap cay*, wok-tossed vegetables with rice.

Pura Luhur Uluwatu

Balanced on the edge of a narrow rocky cape on the southwestern edge of the peninsula is the 11th-century, **Pura Luhur Uluwatu** ❼, the 'Lofty Headstone Temple'. Legend has it that the temple is actually a ship turned to stone. It was rebuilt by the Hindu priest Danghyang Nirartha, who came to Bali from Java in the 16th century following the spread of Islam there, and it was from this cliff top that he is believed to have ascended into heaven after completing this last architectural wonder.

The site is particularly sacred to fishermen, who come here to pray to the sea goddess, Dewi Laut. A small shrine with a statue of the priest and flanked by images of Brahma and Vishnu, Hindu gods of creation and life, are in the walled section to the left just as you enter.

The temple has two unusual gates, one a *candi bentar* (split gate) featuring relief carvings of birds topped by curved wings, and the other an arched structure with a monster face. Both gates are guarded on each side by two statues of Ganesha, the elephant-headed overcomer of obstacles and symbol of success. A part of this long, narrow temple broke away and fell into the sea during the early 1900s, a premonition, it is said, of the impending Dutch massacre of Badung's royal family who had always maintained it. Numerous repairs were made over the years, most recently in the late 1990s after the shrines were struck by lightning. Many people interpreted this as an omen of the immense changes arising from the Asian economic crisis.

The views from here at sunset are spellbinding, with fishing boats dotting the Indian Ocean. If you're lucky you might see turtles, dugong, manta rays and even whales swimming in the waters below.

Above from far left: Pasar Badung, Denpasar; Padang Padang beach, the Bukit; the Pura Luhur Uluwatu is balanced on this rocky cliff top.

Kuta and Seminyak

While Kuta and Seminyak are not stop-overs on this tour, both sit within the Bandung regency, north of the airport and southwest of Denpasar and therefore cannot go without a mention. If you're looking for shopping, fine dining and a pulsating nightlife, you may like to consider making Seminyak your beach side base, with Kuta a cheaper, less sophisticated option. Kuta, once a quiet fishing village, became the victim of years of unplanned development after being discovered by surfers in the 1960s. Nowadays, this hotchpotch of family-run guesthouses, bars, cafés, nightclubs, handicraft shops, surf emporia, money changers, beauty parlours and second-hand bookstores has a beach-party atmosphere. Trendy Seminyak, on the other hand, lays claim to the highest concentration of gourmet restaurants on the island, as well as numerous cocktail bars, nightspots, spas, designer boutiques, luxury villas and five-star hotels, that draw a glamorous crowd of visitors.

Above from left:
kecak dance performed at Pura Luhur Uluwatu; *barong* mask, Puri Saren.

Monkey Business

The area around the temple is inhabited by a band of mischievous monkeys, who snatch unguarded items, so don't wear a hat, sunglasses, dangling earrings or anything else that can be yanked away from you. A traditional **kecak dance performance** takes place here daily at 6pm (charge). Performed by around 100 male dancers, who are bare chested and hypnotically chant '*cak cak cak*', the dance depicts a battle in which Prince Rama is helped to defeat the evil King Ravana by the monkey-like Vanara – hence it is sometimes called the monkey dance.

Uluwatu Beach

An alternative idea for sunset is to drive out of the temple car park and turn left. Follow the road to the end, and walk down the steps to the line of cliff-edge *warungs* (food stalls/cafés). En route, check out **Uluwatu Beach** by descending more steep steps to the left. The beach has sand reminiscent of golden-brown sugar, and is accessible at low tide through a cave. Afterwards relax in one of the many surfer hangouts on the cliff above and watch a spectacular sunset over an ice cold beer. You'll have a great view of the surfers, only the most proficient of whom dare to ride these waves.

JIMBARAN BAY

To end the tour, return along the main road leading back to the tourist centres. Stop at the beautiful crescent-shaped **Jimbaran Bay** ❽ and feast on grilled fresh seafood at one of the seafood cafés on the beach between the Four Seasons Resort and the airport. It's difficult to distinguish between the cafés, but a consistently good one is **Menega Café**, see ⑪③. For a more upmarket dining experience, check out **PJs**, see ⑪④, at the Four Seasons Resort.

Alternatively, if you're staying anywhere near Seminyak or Kerobokan, visit the street colloquially known as 'Eat Street', where you will be spoilt for choice. One of the most popular restaurants there is **Sarong**, see ⑪⑤.

Food and Drink 🍴

③ MENEGA CAFÉ
Jl Four Seasons, Muaya Beach, Jimbaran; tel: 0361-705888/mobile: 0812-39-33539; daily 11am–11pm; $$–$$$
Menega is one of Jimbaran's many seafood cafés, where fresh fish is displayed on ice for you to select. Minstrels serenade you as you enjoy your meal.

④ PJs
Four Seasons Resort, Jimbaran Bay; tel: 0361-701010; daily 11am–10pm; $$$$
PJs, the charming beach-side restaurant at the Four Seasons, Jimbaran, comprises a trio of open-sided pavilions elevated above the sandy shore. The menu offers gourmet pizzas, seafood, oven-roasted duck breast and grilled steaks, and desserts including passionfruit-cream cheesecake.

⑤ SARONG
Jl Petitenget No. 19X, Kerobokan; tel: 0361-737809; www.sarongbali.com; daily 7pm–midnight; $$$–$$$$
The sumptuous quirkiness of Sarong makes it feel so cosy that you could be mistaken for thinking you've walked into someone's home. The menu offers 'classics with a twist' from China, Thailand, Malaysia and India. Reserve.

UBUD HIGHLIGHTS

With so much to see around Ubud, this full-day driving and walking tour has been designed to touch on a variety of sights and activities ranging from Balinese culture, art and history to scenic beauty and wildlife.

Ubud is Bali's cultural hub, a royal village situated at the confluence of two rivers on the southern edge of the island's cool mountainous foothills. A haven for local and foreign artists since the 1930s, it is the island's centre for fine arts and dance. In the surrounding villages you can watch the island's most accomplished painters, stonemasons, woodcarvers, mask makers and silversmiths at work.

CENTRAL UBUD

Ubud Market

Aim for an early start of 7–7.30am (breakfast is scheduled for later) to ensure that you experience the busy **Ubud Market ①** (Jl Raya Ubud)

> **DISTANCE** 14km (9 miles) driving and 2km (1¼ miles) for the ridge walk
> **TIME** A full day
> **START** Ubud Market
> **END** Petulu or Puri Saren Ubud
> **POINTS TO NOTE**
> This tour offers a mix of walking and driving. You can either organise a car and driver for the day or use transport men on the street as and when you need them. Remember to negotiate a price before you set out and make sure the driver waits for you if you opt to visit Petulu at the end of the tour. Wear comfortable walking shoes.

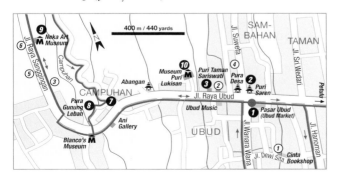

Above from left:
two market scenes at Pasar Ubud; *barong* mask and costume, Puri Saren.

Daluman Drink
The *daluman* stall in Ubud's market serves a thick jelly-like drink formed from the health-giving leaves of the daluman vine. Apparently, it's full of vitamins and good for pregnant women; it tastes quite good, although the slimy texture can take some getting used to.

before much of the fresh produce is whisked away to make room for tourist-oriented handicrafts. If you want to go shopping, plan to go back another day because you won't want to be carrying your purchases around with you on this tour. As you walk through the narrow alleys, look out for the *daluman* stall, where the market's most respected lady mixologist prepares an ominous-looking dark green concoction *(see margin left)*. If you sit at her trestle table, she will blend the mixture with a swirl of coconut milk, a drizzle of liquid palm sugar and a flourish that will convince you it's okay to drink. Look out,

too, for the women serving vegetarian *bubur* – rice porridge slapped on a banana leaf and topped with roasted coconut, sprouts, greens and spicy *sambal* (chilli-based sauce).

Royal Palace

When you come out of the market, cross the street and peer in at the courtyard of **Puri Saren ❷** (corner of Jl Raya Ubud and Jl Suweta; free), the royal palace and home to the Sukawati royal family, one of several royal families in Bali. The public are welcome to stroll around during daylight hours, although there are no information signs. Built in the late 19th century, the palace is formed of a series of splendid pavilions with richly carved doors and incongruous colonial-era European furniture.

By now, you may be ready for a hearty breakfast. **Kafe Batan Waru**, see ⓘ①, serves classy fare such as eggs Benedict on English muffins and wholegrain blueberry pancakes with maple syrup. To get there, go south down Jl Wanara Wana (Monkey Forest Road), opposite the palace, then take the first left into Jl Dewi Sita, where you will find the restaurant after about 250m/yds on the left-hand side. Alternatively, **Café Lotus**, see ⓘ②, is 100m/yds west of the palace on Jl Raya Ubud, the main road. It has a romantic outlook over the beautiful lotus pond of **Pura Taman Sariswati ❸**, a temple built in the 1950s and dedicated to Dewi Saraswati,

History of Art in Bali

Art is omnipresent in Bali, finding its roots in the symbolically decorative adornment of palaces and temples, making it inseparable from courtly life and spiritual practice. For centuries, artists, artisans and craftsmen worked under the patronage of the priests and the ruling classes, decorating the royal courts with carved wooden panels, paintings, silken wall hangings and stone sculptures. These artists of old never signed their work – paintings were produced collaboratively and anonymously, with the men usually living close together in artists' villages.

Things changed in the 1920s and 1930s, with the arrival of avant-garde foreign artists, such as Walter Spies, Rudolf Bonnet, Arie Smit *(see p.38)* and Adrien-Jean Le Mayeur *(see p.29)*, who encouraged individual freedom of expression, while also introducing Western painting concepts. A second movement occurred in the early 1960s, when Arie Smit encouraged the artists of Penestanan to explore and experiment with vivid colours and simpler abstract forms.

the goddess of learning, wisdom and the arts. Note the 3m (10ft) high statue here of Jero Gede Macaling, the demon lord of epidemics and pestilence.

RIDGE WALK

The next part of this tour is a delightful walk along the Campuhan Ridge, but to reach the starting point on the main road near **Kedewatan** ❹ (on the west side of Ubud), you will need a vehicle and driver, or a *bemo* (public minivan). Kedewatan village is famous for the fuzzy red fruit known as rambutan or buluan, similar to lychee. Buy some of these sweet fruits if they are in season, along with some bottled water.

From Kedewatan, follow the sign to **Pura Puncak Payogan** ❺, the 'Summit Temple of Meditation' at Payogan, where, during the 8th century, the holy man Resi Markandeya meditated after coming from Java, having followed a bright light to Bali. Just to the right, a narrow paved road winds down a river valley and up the other side to **Bangkiansidem** ❻ (Ant's Waist), named because this village lies on a narrow ridge between two broader sections.

The road ends at a paved footpath, so if you hire a car with a driver, ask him to wait at the staircase near the eastern end of the bridge in **Campuhan** ❼. Continue on the path for a leisurely 1km (½-mile) stroll with magnificent vistas of the countryside

Food and Drink
① KAFE BATAN WARU
Jl Dewi Sita, tel: 0361-9775288; www.baligoodfood.com/Batanwaru.asp; daily 8am–midnight; $$
Styled after a colonial teahouse with tea chairs and a collection of rare lithographs and prints, this restaurants serves authentic Indonesian dishes such as Grandma Atik's 'Ikan Acar Kuning' (fish steaks in a turmeric sauce with peppers and pickled garlic), international food and superb breakfasts.

② CAFÉ LOTUS
Jl Raya Ubud; tel: 0361-975660; www.lotus-restaurants.com/cafe-lotus-ubud; daily 8.30am–11pm; $$
This landmark restaurant has a gorgeous outlook over a lotus pond; a frame of gnarled frangipani trees with a temple backdrop completes the picture. Serves delicious pastas and desserts, as well as energy-booster drinks.

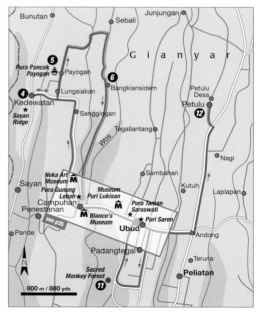

spreading out before you. The hillsides are covered with *alang alang* or *ambengan*, the grass that is used for thatching. Down below, you may be able to see people cutting out blocks of *paras* rock from the river banks. This compressed clay and volcanic ash is mostly used for carving statues and temple adornment.

Campuhan

On a clear day, you can see Gunung Agung *(see p.54)*, Bali's most revered volcano, rising majestically in the east – this was the source of the light that

Resi Markandeya followed. At this point, take a look back at the view of palm trees and mountains.

The walk ends in Campuhan at **Pura Gunung Lebah ➑**, the 'Temple of the Low Mountain' (Gunung Batur), dedicated to the lake goddess of Danau Batur. Resi Markandeya built his home at this holy site. Two rivers meet at Campuhan, meaning confluence, and the Balinese hold purification rituals here.

From the river, take the staircase up to the bridge. This is where your driver will be waiting, if you have hired one.

Balinese Temples

The temple or *pura* is the focus of the spiritual activity of every Balinese Hindu community on the island. They are specially designed without roofs to allow the gods easy access between the worlds, with the gates and walls serving to keep impure and evil influences away. Most villages on the island have at least three temples, and every home has a *merajan* (shrine) or *sanggah kemulan* (house temple). There are nine *kahyangan jagat* or directional temples in the province, and these are of major importance because they protect the entire island and its people. Other temples may be particularly significant because of their strategic cliff-top or lakeside locations, their history, or their architectural beauty.

NEKA ART MUSEUM

Next en route is the **Neka Art Museum ➒** (Jl Raya Sangingan; tel: 0361-975074; www.museumneka.com; daily 9am–5pm; charge), which is just under 1.5km (¾ mile) up the hill to the west. It was founded in 1976 by Suteja Neka, a schoolteacher-turned-art-collector. Here, a series of pavilions amid manicured gardens presents an outstanding collection of artwork showing the different historical styles of Balinese painting. Works by foreign artists, especially the Dutch-born Arie Smit, are a highlight, as are photographs from the 1930s. Look out for works by the late great Javanese artist, Abdul Aziz, whose subjects appear to lean out of their frames. Every piece has an informative label, so allow one or two

hours to learn more about Balinese art and culture.

Afterwards, stop for lunch at **Indus**, see ⑨③, just 500m/yds down the hill from the art museum. The home cooking at this popular restaurant is superb, and the view from the open terrace of the mountain, the ridge and the river valley is magnificent.

MUSEUM PURI LUKISAN

If you have time and you would like to see some more art, drop by the **Museum Puri Lukisan** ❿ (Jl Raya Ubud; tel: 0361-971159; www.museumpuri lukisan.com; daily 9am–5pm; charge), set in attractive gardens with lotus ponds. To reach it, head east back towards the town for about 2km (1¼ miles), and you will find the museum set back from the road on the left-hand side. Founded in 1956, it features works by Balinese painters and carvers of the Pitamaha (Noble Aspiration), a famous artists' association in Ubud, which was active from 1936 to 1942.

SACRED MONKEY FOREST

A fun activity, especially if you have kids, is a stroll through the **Sacred Monkey Forest** ⓫ (Padangtegal; tel 0361-971034/972774; daily 8am–6pm; charge). You'll need transport to get there, and it's a good idea to ask your driver to wait for you. From Puri Lukisan Museum, turn left and follow the road back to the royal palace and market. You can't turn into Monkey Forest Road in a four-wheeled vehicle because it is a one-way street, so instead take the first turning after the market into Jl Hanoman and follow the road all the way down to the bottom of the hill, where you will see the entrance. This holy area and important ecological reserve is home to a band of about 300 long-tailed grey Balinese macaques. They can be very mischievous, but they are interesting to observe, especially with their young. There are vendors on hand selling bananas with which to feed the birds.

Other attractions here include three temples, which are accessible via the paved pathways: the holy bathing

Above from far left:
Ngaben (Funeral Ceremony) by da Bagus Made at Museum Puri Lukisan; the museum's gardens.

Food and Drink ⑨
③ INDUS
Jl Raya Sanggingan; tel: 0361-977684; www.casalunabali.com/indus-restaurant; daily 7.30am–11pm; $$
An Ubud favourite, with stunning views of the Tjampuhan River valley and Mt Agung from its terraces and cool open-sided interior. Serves healthy Asian cuisine, including Indian chickpea curry, and Indonesian *nasi campur*, comprised of red rice and a selection of vegetables, meat or fish, and other accompaniments such as the fried soya bean cakes known as *tempe*. There is also a small art gallery on the premises.

Above: *Waiting to Dance* (1983) and *Rama's promise to Sita* (1976), both by Abdul Aziz at the Neka Art Museum.

Sacred Herons of Petulu

Local legend tells that there were no herons in the village of Petulu until after the political backlash that followed the attempted coup of 1965, when tens of thousands of men and women were murdered. Ask any of the elders in the village, and they will tell you that the birds appeared after one of the worst of the massacres, and are believed to be the souls of the slaughtered.

temple (down a long flight of steps next to a river); the important Pura Dalem Agung Padangtegal with its ornately carved gate; and Pura Prajapati, the funeral or cremation temple.

PETULU

You will now need a driver to take you to the tiny village of **Petulu** ⓬; aim to arrive around 5.30pm. To get there, head back up Monkey Forest Road, turn right and follow the main road to the end, where there is a big statue.

Turn left and head up the hill. The road to Petulu is on the left-hand side after about 2km (1¼ miles), heralded by a painting of a white heron. Another 1km (½ mile) brings you into the village, which is famous because every evening at sunset thousands of white Javan pond herons *(see margin, left)* and plumed egrets come to roost for the night. It's a spectacular sight, as the flocks of birds fill the sky before landing, squabbling over prime perches and turning the tree tops white. Village tradition dictates that the birds

Right: tourist feeding a monkey.

should not be disturbed during their roosting, but you can sit at a simple viewing platform, and drink cold Bintang beers or soft drinks as you watch.

DANCES AND DINNER

An alternative to the Petulu herons is an early evening Balinese dance performance in the courtyard of Puri Saren, the Royal Palace (corner of Jl Raya Ubud and Jl Suweta; starts at 7.30pm; charge), by far the best and most dramatic setting for the performing arts in Ubud. One of the most famous dances is the *legong* dance *(see margin, right)*, which is performed here every evening along with some other dances.

Dinner options in the town are plentiful. **Terazo**, see ⑪④, on Jl Suweta, near the palace, is a popular hang-out, while **Mozaic**, see ⑪⑤, located near Neka Art Museum, offers gourmet dining. Also on this stretch is the well-known **Naughty Nuri's**, see ⑪⑥, which is evocative of an English pub, with a daily barbecue.

Above from far left: traditional dance, Pura Gunung Lebah, Ubud; residents of Monkey Forest; *legong* performance, Municipal Hall, Ubud.

Legong Dance

The *legong* dance – a quintessential display of Balinese grace and femininity, performed by three young girls – is the most refined of all the temple dances. There are various forms of this dance, the most common being the *legong karaton*, based on a classic 12th-century tale from Java about a princess held captive by a wicked king.

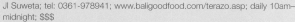

Food and Drink

④ TERAZO

Jl Suweta; tel: 0361-978941; www.baligoodfood.com/terazo.asp; daily 10am–midnight; $$$

This semi open-air restaurant and bar is flanked by ponds with dining on two levels under a soaring roof. The contemporary Asian and Mediterranean-style cuisine here is slightly upmarket, and the vibe is friendly and casual yet hip.

⑤ MOZAIC

Jl Raya Sanggingan; tel: 0361-975768; www.mozaic-bali.com; Tue–Sun 6pm–midnight; $$$$

Mozaic is the only restaurant in Indonesia to have received the accolade of entry in the worldwide guide *Les Grandes Tables du Monde*. Tables spill out into a romantic candlelit garden, and the eclectic cuisine, with its French-style presentation, attracts discerning gourmets. Chef-owner Chris Salans believes that fixed menus are restrictive, so his ever-changing list of creations is reprinted on a daily basis, as dishes evolve, disappear and return in accordance with market availability. The best way to sample the cuisine is through the seven-course tasting menu that may include delights such as rosemary-braised ocean trout fillet and spiced organic pumpkin purée, in a roasted-onion Spanish saffron emulsion.

⑥ NAUGHTY NURI'S

Jl Raya Sanggingan; tel: 0361-977547; daily 9am–11pm; $$

A favourite with Ubud's expats, drawn by the potent Martinis, this street-side semi open-air *warung*-style pub is always busy. You can order steaks, lamb chops, ribs and sausages from the barbecue, or choose from a limited selection of Indonesian dishes from the menu.

BATUR AND KINTAMANI

In this tour, a good day trip from Ubud, highlights include descending into a volcanic caldera, climbing the active volcano in the centre of the caldera or just relaxing in the hot springs at the crater lake.

DISTANCE 19km (12 miles)
TIME A full day if you climb the volcano or a more leisurely half day if you don't.
START Kintamani
END Pura Puncak Penulisan
POINTS TO NOTE
If you plan to climb the volcano, leave as early as possible to avoid the midday heat (you may prefer to do the sunrise trek, which begins around 4am). Wear good walking shoes, dress comfortably and bring hats, suncream and bottled water. Don't attempt this during the rainy season (Nov–Mar), as it can get dangerously slippery. Batur and the Kintamani area are located about 30km (18 miles) from Ubud, so this tour could follow on from the Ubud Highlights trip *(see p.35)* and the Pejeng and Bangli tour *(see p.50)*.

Kintamani Dogs
Hailing from this region is Bali's only officially recognised breed of dog. Prized for their long furry coats (especially if they are white), Kintamani dogs are fiercely independent with a distinctive character that sets them apart from the average Balinese street dog. They dig holes in which to nest their young, and some even live in small caves among the boulders around Kintamani.

Tourists flock to Kintamani, typically to enjoy an Indonesian buffet lunch at one of the many panoramic restaurants that overhang the ancient volcanic crater rim there. The caldera is 14km (8¾ miles) across at its widest diameter, and in the middle is the black cone of Gunung Batur, a volcano that puffs out steam and has erupted more than 20 times in the last 200 years. At its foot is the crescent-shaped Danau Batur, the island's largest lake. Its depth has never been recorded, but the lake is the source of most of the rivers in the eastern half of Bali.

PENELOKAN

Take the road north out of Ubud through Payangan and drive 32km (20 miles) up to the village of **Kintamani ❶**, set on the rim of a huge, ancient caldera. Turn right along the scenic road that follows the crater rim for 3km (1¾ miles) to **Penelokan ❷**, meaning 'viewpoint' because of the stunning view of the volcano and the lake below.

At Penelokan, visit **Batur Volcano Museum** (Jl Kintamani, Penelokan; tel: 0366-51152; www.baturmuseum.com; daily 8am–5pm; charge), where you can learn all about volcanic phenomena through information panels, interactive games and computer simulations, as well as three 20-minute films. The museum is fun to visit with children.

TOYA BUNGKAH

Wind 8km (5 miles) down through lava fields to **Toya Bungkah** ❸. This lakeside fishing village, one of eight *bintang danu* (stars of the lake), has grown as an accommodation centre and the main start point for treks up Gunung Batur.

GUNUNG BATUR

Gunung Batur is 1,717m (5,635ft) high, but the upper cone is only 700m (2,275ft) above the level of the lake and can be climbed and descended in a few hours. A local cartel actively discourages independent trekkers by not allowing people to hike alone, so you will need to hire a licensed guide. 'Official' fees for guides are high, but much cheaper deals can be negotiated at some of the guesthouses and restaurants at the lake.

The strange landscape is punctuated with bizarre hillocks and a series of craters with jets of white steam puffing out of small holes. On a clear day, you will be rewarded with a beautiful view of the lake, Mt Abang, Mt Agung, the distant sea and Mt Rinjani in Lombok. The surface is loose and sandy here, and at the top there's a warm crust of ground, so be careful where you tread. Ask your guide to prepare a meal of baked bananas and hard-boiled eggs cooked to perfection in the natural heat belching from the belly of the volcano (you may need to ask them in advance to do this).

DANAU BATUR

After the descent, the hot springs at Toya Bungkah, on the shore of **Danau Batur**, are perfect for easing aching limbs – though the rest of the lake is cold, the water here can be close to scalding. Frequented mostly by locals, the public bathing spot is free but polluted, since many people use soap. Recommended is the **Tirta Sanjiwani** (daily 8am–5pm; charge), with two hot-spring pools plus a regular swimming pool in a lovely garden above the lake.

Afterwards, have lunch at nearby **Nyoman Mawa 'Under the Volcano'**, see ⓘ① *(p.44)*, which has excellent crispy fried fish *(mujahir),* served with chilli-onion relish. (Alternatively, back up on the rim are restaurants catering to busloads of tourists; one of the best is at **Lakeview Hotel**, see ⓘ②, *p.44*.)

Above: the view from the aptly named Lakeview Hotel restaurant.

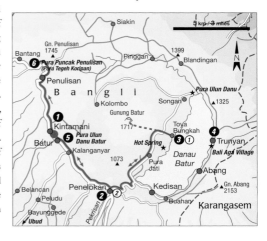

Above from left:
prayers at Pura
Ulun Danu Batur;
Goa Gajah.

Ring of Fire

There are some
500 volcanoes in
Indonesia, of which
129 are considered to
be active and part of
the Pacific Ring
of Fire – a zone of
frequent earthquakes
and volcanic
eruptions that
encircles the basin
of the Pacific Ocean.
The number of active
volcanoes in
Indonesia is equal
to 13 percent of
the world's total.

TRUNYAN

Look across the lake and on the eastern
shore you will see the isolated village of
Trunyan ❹. The residents are Bali Aga
people, who inhabited the island long
before the 14th-century Majapahit
invasion and sought refuge from impe-
rialistic strangers. Today, the people of
Trunyan still retain a social order
aligned with ancient traditions. Among
their rules is that cremation should not
be practised here. Instead, in a shadowy
cemetery some 500m/yds outside the
village and accessible only by boat, the
bodies of the dead are wrapped in cloth
and simply left in bamboo cages on the
ground. Strangely, there is no smell, due
to the presence of a Taru Menyan tree,
believed to produce a fragrant odour,
while its roots, beneath the bodies, baf-
flingly prevent putrefaction. Only the
brave visit Trunyan. Most visitors are
discouraged by tales of touts demanding
extortionate boat fares that increase
halfway across the lake, while many tour
guides claim that taking tourists there
is more trouble than it's worth.

TEMPLE TOUR

Now return to Penelokan via the rim
and drive 4km (2½ miles) north to **Pura
Ulun Danu Batur** ❺ (donation), Bali's
second most important temple complex. Unlike other temples in Bali, it is
always open and has a permanent staff
of 24 priests; selected as children by a
virgin priestess, they serve for life. The
temple was relocated here in 1926 when
lava flows destroyed the original one at
the edge of the lake below. The largest
temple, Pura Penataran Agung Batur, is
dedicated to the lake goddess. The gates
are towering architectural masterpieces,
and there is an air of mystery in the late
afternoon, when mists roll in.

Pura Puncak Penulisan

Drive a further 3km (1¾ miles) uphill
past Kintamani to **Pura Puncak
Penulisan** ❻ (also known as Pura
Tegeh Koripan; open daylight hours;
donation), Bali's highest temple, and
climb the long staircase to this ancient
'High Life Temple' shrouded by mists.
Here, you'll see statues of ancient deified kings and queens, carved between
the 10th and 14th centuries. On clear
days, the views are spectacular.

Food and Drink 🍴

① NYOMAN MAWA 'UNDER THE VOLCANO'

Jl Batur Tengah, Toya Bungkah; tel: 0366-51166; daily
7am–9pm; $
This restaurant is linked to a small hotel, and situated lakeside in an open-sided pavilion with the volcano towering
above. Serves simple international dishes and local fare
including the house speciality of sweet fish from the lake.

② LAKEVIEW HOTEL

Penelokan; tel: 0366-51394; daily 7am–10pm; $–$$
The Lakeview Hotel restaurant is perched on a mountain
ridge with awesome views from picture windows and a
narrow terrace that offers alfresco dining. Serves a daily
buffet breakfast including delicious banana fritters, followed
from 11am daily by a traditional Indonesian buffet.

BEDULU, TAMPAKSIRING AND TEGALLALANG

4

*This busy day tour covers an area southeast and east of Ubud. Sights include
a holy cave, two temple complexes, funerary monuments, holy springs,
steeply terraced rice fields, woodcarving shops and the Elephant Safari Park.*

This tour begins 5km (3 miles) southeast of Ubud, in a region heavy with
ancient archaeological sites and old
temples. It then heads to the Tampa-
siring area, where highlights include a
cluster of ancient temples, before con-
tinuing to Tegallalang (Grass Fields),
known for its rice terraces that spill
down a river gorge and home to a
family-friendly Elephant Safari Park.

AROUND BEDULU

After an early breakfast, head south
out of Ubud through Peliatan. From
here, follow the main road as it turns
east for 2km (1¼ miles) to **Bedulu ❶**
(or Bedahulu) and Goa Gajah. Bedulu
village is positioned on the banks of
the Petanu River. Despite its small size
it is steeped in history and surrounded
by some of Bali's most notable and
ancient wonders. Ubud's best known
artist, I Gusti Nyoman Lempad, was
born here in 1862 and lived to be 116;
he built and carved many of Bedulu's
temple gates and shrines. The *kecak*
dance *(see p.34)* was also devised in
Bedulu in 1930s.

> **DISTANCE** 40km (25 miles)
> **TIME** A full day
> **START** Bedulu
> **END** Taro
> **POINTS TO NOTE**
> There are a lot of sights to cover, so
> you may choose to focus only on
> some of them. The elephant park
> could be omitted at the end, but it
> is highly recommended, especially
> for families with children. Bring hats,
> suncream and bottled water.

Goa Gajah

Descend the steps into the **Goa Gajah
❷** (Elephant Cave; daily 9am–5pm;
charge), which dates from the 11th
century and is carved out of solid rock.
Just above the cave entrance is a mon-
strous head, known as Bhoma and
believed to frighten away evil.

The interior is in a T-shape. At the
left (western) end is a four-armed stone
image of Ganesha, the elephant-headed
Hindu god and remover of obstacles,
after whom the cave is named. To the
right are three *lingga* (phallic images of

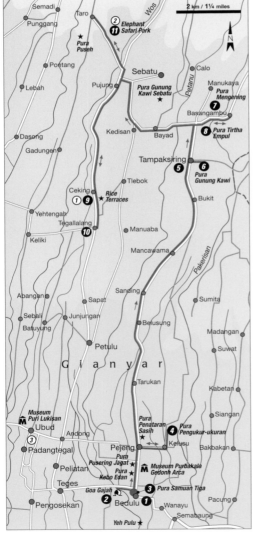

Shiva, Hindu god of destruction and reincarnation) with eight smaller ones around each, all on a common base and carved from a single stone.

In front of the cave is a bathing place with steps leading down to separate areas for men and women. The place is no longer used for bathing, however. Water pours out of jars held by four voluptuous female stone figures flanking two chunky males, whose upper halves once stood outside the cave entrance. In 1954 a Dutch archaeologist excavated the area and uncovered the matching lower halves of the statues. Behind this is Pura Taman, a modern temple with a shrine in a pond.

South of the bathing place are steps leading down to a river. Cross the bridge and you will see nearby the remains of a relief carving of Buddhist temple structures.

Pura Samuan Tiga

Return to the main road and continue east for 1km (½ mile) beyond the intersection to **Pura Samuan Tiga** ❸ (daylight hours; donation). This vast 'temple of the meeting of the three parties' stages an 11-day ceremony during the 10th full moon; it is the third most important temple in Bali and was the state temple of the Warmadewa dynasty, which ruled up to the 14th century. The name may refer to the blend of animism, Buddhism and Hinduism practised in Bali today.

Above from far
left: Pura Samuan
Tiga, and festival
preparations therein;
carvings on coconut
shells, Tampaksiring.

There are dozens of shrines here, built on a series of terraces; some house ancient stone figures of deities and phallic images. The temple has undergone continuous renovation since 1994 but still retains an atmosphere of awe and power. Festivals here involve huge processions, ritual dances and mock battles.

Under a soaring banyan tree are three multi-tiered brick-and-stone *meru* (pagodas), structures usually made of wood and thatching found in most Balinese temples. From north to south (left to right), these are dedicated to the deities of the lakes, wealth and sea, representing the upper, middle and lower realms of the spiritual world. People usually pray here for material success. Some pavilions house ancient sculptures of the goddess of death – Durga trampling the buffalo demon, phallic representations of the god of destruction, Shiva, and other Hindu deities. The main gate leading to the terraces is guarded by a face of Bhoma to frighten away evil.

Pura Pengukur-ukuran

Continue on the narrow road going east past the temple and follow it north for 4km (2½ miles) through Petemon and Sawagunung all the way up to the 12th-century temple complex of **Pura Pengukur-ukuran ❹** (daylight hours; donation). Rich carvings adorn the walls and gates of this so-called 'Temple of Measurements'. Walk carefully down a steep flight of enormous stone steps to the river; this is a quiet place with an air of mystery and a good place to cool off. There are three small niches nearby, one with some statues. Examine the arrangement carefully, for villagers say that if you look again later, the figures may have shifted places by themselves.

A small path downstream leads you up to the main road. Backtrack 2km (1¼ miles) south and turn right at a junction that takes you the same distance west. The road emerges at the main intersection in Pejeng.

TAMPAKSIRING

From here, turn right and continue north for 13km (8 miles) uphill to

Rice Farming

The intensely productive *sawah* (rice fields) of Bali are a thousand years old, as are the democratic irrigation cooperatives, or *subak*, that manage them. The substance of rural life is dependent on the accuracy of the water flow as it is diverted from the rivers and steams that gush from the crater lakes in Bali's central highlands. Through ancient, yet sophisticated, systems of aquatic engineering, including canals, tunnels and bamboo pipes, combined with elaborate social structures, the *subak* control the flow of water to ensure its even distribution to Bali's farmers. Using gravity, water is channelled into the uppermost *sawah* before flowing downhill to supply each farm in turn. The *subak* are not only responsible for the upkeep and maintenance of the channels, tunnels and aqueducts, but also the coordination of the rice planting.

Taro Village

The ancient village of Taro marks the centre of the island. According to legend, this was where the 8th-century itinerant Javanese priest Rsi Markandya was sent by the gods on a mission to establish a settlement in the forest. It is also where Bali's sacred albino buffalo comes from.

Tampaksiring ❺. This district is home to numerous woodcarvers and the Presidential Palace (one of three in Indonesia), which was built in the late 1950s for President Soekarno and is now used as an occasional presidential residence. There are some interesting spots to visit in this pretty area, which is surrounded by rice terraces.

You'll see a sign on your right for **Pura Gunung Kawi** ❻ (daily 9am–5pm; charge), a blinding green water canyon surrounded by swaying fields of indigenous Balinese rice, known as 'Padi Bali'. Approached via a long, steep run of steps, this is one of the prettiest places on the island. Gaze in wonder at 10 ancient royal shrines dedicated to 11th-century Balinese royalty, carved out of the solid rock face of the gorge of the Pakerisan River. This 'Mountain Temple of Poets' is a memorial to King Anak Wungsu of the Warmadewa dynasty. They are not tombs, however, as none of the ashes of the cremated bodies were deposited here. The 7m (23ft) high carvings resemble 9th-century Javanese *candi* (memorial shrines).

A cluster of four *candi* on the west bank are monuments to the king's minor consorts, while five more across the river are for the king, queen and important family members. Water flows through small channels and pours out from spouts into a pool that once served as a royal bath.

Located nearby is a cluster of niches and enclosed rooms, also cut from solid rock; these may once have been a Buddhist monastery. Remove your footwear before entering.

Pura Mengening

Return to the main road and continue 1km (½ mile) north to a crossroads and turn right. A sign on your right indicates a road to **Pura Mengening** ❼ (daylight hours; donation), a small 'Clear Water Temple', with a holy spring under a banyan tree. Nearby is a larger, newly renovated temple with a restored ancient building inside

Food and Drink

① KAMPUNG CAFÉ

Ceking, Tegallalang; tel: 0361-901201; daily 9am–10pm; $$
This rustic restaurant clings to the edge of the Sapat river valley, with fine views of the rice terraces down the side of the gorge. Fresh ingredients are used to create superb Indonesian and Western dishes including 'ayam sabal sereh', spicy chicken with lemongrass on a bed of stir-fried water spinach and seared fillet of *mahi mahi* on spinach fettucine with creamy garlic ginger sauce.

② ELEPHANT PARK RESTAURANT

Jl Elephant Park Taro, Tegallalang; tel: 0361-721480; daily 8am–6pm; $$
The restaurant inside the elephant park overlooks the lake where the elephants bathe. Serves good-quality Western and Asian cuisine. Dinner for Safari Park Lodge guests only.

③ LAMAK

Monkey Forest Road, Ubud; tel: 0361-974668; www.lamakbali.com; daily 11am–11pm; $$$–$$$$
This fine-dining restaurant is decorated in a funky, flamboyant take on the traditional. The menu is a marriage of Asian food with recipes from the south of France, the Mediterranean and Asia, such as quail *saltimbocca* on red wine risotto with garlic gravy. Dine alfresco or in an air-conditioned area inside.

resembling the temple facades at Pura Gunung Kawi.

Pura Tirtha Empul

Return to the main road and continue to nearby **Pura Tirtha Empul** ❽ (daily 8am–6pm; charge), a 10th-century holy spring and temple. Possessing magical powers and believed to be the elixir of immortality, the gin-clear freshwater springs bubble up into a large tank within the temple and gush out through water spouts into a bathing pool, where elaborate carvings adorn the lichen-covered walls.

TEGALLALANG

Backtrack 500m/yds to a small cross-roads and instead of bearing left (south) on the main road, go west for 3km (2 miles) until you meet the main Tegallalang–Ubud road. If a late lunch, spectacular views and handicraft shopping is on your agenda, turn left and head south, stopping after 4.5km (2¾ miles) at **Kampung Café**, see ⑪①, in **Ceking** ❾ to eat and take in the dramatic view of rice terraces.

Continue south for 1km (½ mile) to take a closer look at this spectacular sculpted landscape in **Tegallalang** ❿. This is a 5km (3-mile) long street of woodcarving workshops and simple wholesale outlets, where you will see wooden handicrafts and bamboo wind-chimes galore, at half the price you would pay in Kuta.

Elephant Safari Park

Alternatively, if you would prefer to spend the afternoon interacting with elephants, turn right at the point where you meet the main Tegallalang–Ubud road and head north for 500m/yds. Turn left at the junction and follow the signs to the **Elephant Safari Park** ⓫ (Jl Elephant Park Taro, Tegallalang; tel: 0361-721480; daily 8am–6pm; charge), which enjoys a cool jungle setting next to the remote, historic village of **Taro** *(see margin, left)*.

The park provides sanctuary for 30 Sumatran elephants *(see margin, right)*, including three babies born at the park in 2009. Here, adults and children can enjoy the wonderful and unforgettable experience of meeting, hand-feeding, touching, stroking and observing these amazing, highly intelligent creatures, rescued from the Indonesian island of Sumatra. You can even ride the elephants on a safari tour through the park – children love this – and watch elephant talent shows.

A great asset for Bali, the park is regarded as the best of its kind in the world and is an exceptional example of ecotourism. There is a restaurant here, see ⑪②, which makes a good alternative venue for lunch. You can also stay overnight here and wake up with the elephants at the **Safari Park Lodge**, or return to Ubud for dinner, where a good choice might be **Lamak**, see ⑪③.

Above from far left: intricate carvings on cattle bones, Tampaksiring; Tegallalang rice terraces; the holy springs at Pura Tirtha Empul.

Sumatran Elephants
The Sumatran elephant – the world's smallest and possibly oldest elephant species – once roamed freely in a rich, diverse habitat untouched by man. Over the last few decades, however, the population of this little-known species has rapidly and tragically declined, due to increased illegal logging and the destruction of rainforests to make way for palm-oil plantations. This leaves the Sumatran elephant as one of the rarest, most highly endangered elephant species.

PEJENG AND BANGLI

Highlights on this tour, which heads northeast of Ubud, include the world's largest kettledrum, erotic temple sculptures, an archaeological museum, dramatic relief carvings and the terraces of an imposing temple.

Moon of Pejeng Gong

Said to be more than 2,000 years old, Pura Pusering Jagat's 'Moon of Pejeng' gong' has a 160cm (63in) diameter head and a height of 187cm (73in), making it the largest, single-cast, bronze kettledrum in the world. Notice that a piece of the base is missing. The story goes that one night, one of the 13 moons (or a wheel from the moon's chariot) fell from the sky and landed in a tree. A thief who was disturbed by the light urinated on it to extinguish the glow. The moon exploded and killed him, then fell to the ground and cracked. The kettledrum is the *sasih* (moon) and is venerated by villagers; offerings are made to it daily but it is never sounded because no one dares touch it.

DISTANCE 31km (19 miles)
TIME A full day
START Pejeng
END Kota Gianyar
POINTS TO NOTE
This trip can follow on from tour 3 *(see p.42)* and done more or less in reverse starting at Bangli. Alternatively, it can be combined (on separate days) with tour 4 *(see p.45)*. Wear comfortable shoes, as there are some steps to climb, although nothing too strenuous. If you are staying in Ubud, you should be able to find a driver in the town. Note that there are no international-standard restaurants or cafés on this route, so you may wish to pack a picnic. Alternatively, stop for a bite at one of the small, basic local *warungs* (stalls) passed en route, although note that the choice at these will be limited.

This tour winds through the ancient Pejeng-Bedulu kingdom, where there are numerous notable relics, and ends in the sleepy town of Bangli, the former capital of another ancient kingdom.

PEJENG

The journey begins in the village of **Pejeng ❶**, 4km (2½ miles) east of Ubud, named after an illustrious kingdom that was concentrated in this area from the 9th to the 14th centuries. Here you will find **Pura Panataran Sasih ❷**, or Temple of the Moon, which contains the celebrated bronze gong, or kettledrum, known as the 'Moon of Pejeng' *(see margin, left)*.

Pura Pusering Jagat

From here it is just a short walk south down the main road to **Pura Pusering Jagat ❸**, a large temple famous for its highly realistic stone *lingga* and *yoni* (images of the male and female sexual organs). Childless couples come here to pray for children. Nearby is a big cylindrical stone vessel carved with images of gods and demons churning the elixir of life in a scene from the 5,000-year-old Hindu epic, the *Mahabaharata*, a tale of intrigue and conflict among kings, demons, gods and sages. A depression in the ground nearby is the navel of this 'Temple of the Navel of the Universe'. Offerings placed here vanish, allegedly reappearing far away at Pura

Dalem Ped on Nusa Penida, off the southeast coast (*see p.80*).

Temple of the Crazy Buffalo

Just down the road is **Pura Kebo Edan** ❹ (daylight hours; donation). This 'Temple of the Crazy Buffalo' is famous for its large 14th-century statue of a masked giant with serpent-entwined legs dancing on a demon. His equally giant penis adorned with stimulating knobs swings to the left, symbolic of the Tantric ritual indulgence of forbidden acts.

Museum Purbakala Gedong Arca

Keep going south a short distance to **Museum Purbakala Gedong Arca** ❺ (Tue–Sun 8.30am–2pm; charge), a small archaeological museum that showcases ancient pre-Hindu artefacts, stone carvings and old Chinese porcelain. The most fascinating exhibits are large stone sarcophagi with curious protruding heads on the upper and lower halves, looking rather like mating turtles. These ancient coffins show that prehistoric Balinese buried their dead before Buddhists and Hindus introduced cremation.

YEH PULU

By car, continue south 3km (2 miles) into Bedulu (Bedahulu) (*see p.45*), crossing the bend in the main road. At the end of the road, walk on a paved path through rice fields to **Yeh Pulu** ❻.

Adorning a rock wall are large narrative relief carvings believed to have been created in the 14th century by the legendary Balinese giant, strongman and master builder, Kebo Iwa, using his fingernails. In the series of images, a man is carrying pots of water, a woman peers out from her house, a horseback rider watches a hunt of wild boars, and a woman grabs the tail of his steed.

KUTRI

Backtrack all the way to the bend in the main road and turn right, heading 2km (1¼ miles) east to **Semabaung**. Turn

Above from far left:
Pura Kehen; the carvings at Yeh Pulu.

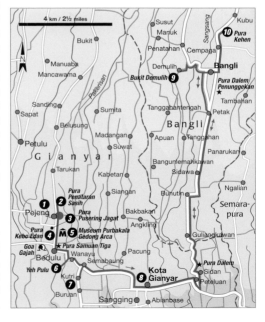

Above from left:
Pura Kehen; the Kerta
Gosa, in Klungkung.

Above: Hindu
ceremonies.

Kul-Kul
The *kul-kul* is a large
wooden bell that
hangs from a high
tower and is used
for calling the *banjar*
(village community).
The different rhythms,
which are known as
tabuh, signify various
messages, from the
news of the death
of a villager to an
emergency such
as a fire or simply
the notification of
a regular meeting.

right again at the traffic lights to reach
nearby **Kutri** ❼, home to a cluster of
three temples: Pura Puseh, Pura Bukit
Dharma, and Pura Kedharman. Climb
the steps up a small hill to see a dramatic statue of Hindu goddess Durga,
with multiple arms holding all sorts of
weapons, slaying a buffalo demon.

BANGLI

The regency and town of Bangli is
located in the foothills of the Batur
volcanic range. Due to its proximity to
Lake Batur, a major source of irrigation water for south and east Bali, the
regency was greatly fought over by
neighbouring rulers. Bangli became
the capital of this Balinese kingdom in
the Balinese Icaka year of 1204.

From here go back to the traffic lights
and bear right, staying on the main road
and heading east for 3km (2 miles). At
the next junction, turn left to reach
Kota Gianyar (Gianyar City) ❽, the
capital of a former powerful kingdom
and famous for its woven textiles. For
now, drive through the town centre –
we'll return here later; after you come
out of the town, take the first turning (a
major junction) on the left, heading
north for 8km (5 miles) to **Bangli**.

Just north of that town, take a
winding road to the right (west) for
1km (½ mile) towards **Bukit Demulih**
❾. This is the 'Hill of No Return', so-
named for its beautiful views, which
will make you reluctant to leave.

Pura Kehen
However, do go back to the main road
and head east to **Pura Kehen** ❿ (daily
9am–5pm; charge), the state temple of
the Bangli kingdom and the second
largest in Bali. It is also one of the
island's most beautiful and impressive
temples, built during the 11th century
and set on a wooded hillside with terraces lined with religious statues. The
imposing entrance, with its fabulously
carved doors depicting grotesque
demons, is flanked by elephant heads,
while the temple itself has dozens of
shrines and an 11-tiered *meru* (pagoda)
dedicated to Shiva. Blue-and-white
Chinese plates are set into the walls,
and the *kul-kul* (*see margin, left*) is
entwined within the branches of a
massive banyan tree.

KOTA GIANYAR

Return to the main road and backtrack
to Kota Gianyar *(see left)*. By late afternoon, the streets by the town market
will be lined with stalls for the night fair.
Browse and try some local food such as
roast suckling pig, fried fish with hot
sauce, smoked chicken and Balinese
sweets, or head back to Ubud *(see p.35)*
for classier restaurant fare.

For a special treat, you may also like
to dine at one of the boutique hotels
on the Ayung River Gorge, such as
Ubud Hanging Gardens or **Four
Seasons Sayan** *(for both, see p.97)*, both
of which have stunning views.

KLUNGKUNG
AND BESAKIH

Visit the former Royal Courts of Justice in Klungkung, then continue to the 'Mother Temple' on the slopes of Bali's highest and holiest mountain, before descending through stunning rice terraces to a weaving village.

The villages of the Klungkung and Karangasem regencies, in the east, are among the most beautiful in Bali. This tour takes you through some of these villages after visiting an historic royal capital, followed by the largest and most sacred site on the island.

KLUNGKUNG

This tour starts in **Klungkung** ❶ (also known as Semarapura), meaning 'happiness' or 'beauty'. The town is the royal capital of Bali's smallest regency and in 1908 was the last kingdom to hold out against the Dutch. The king of Klungkung led 200 hopelessly out-numbered members of his family and court into a *puputan* (ritual suicide), in the face of the Dutch guns. Most of **Puri Semarapura** (Fortress of Love Palace; Klungkung tourist office tel: 0366-21448; daily 9am–5pm; charge) was destroyed at the time of the *puputan*, but in Taman Gili, the gardens of the former palace, the 300-year-old **Kerta Gosa** (Royal Courts of Justice) and **Bale Kembang** (floating pavilion) still stand. Bale

DISTANCE 43km (26 miles)
TIME Half day or a leisurely day
START Klungkung
END Sidemen
POINTS TO NOTE
There's nothing too arduous about this tour, apart from the steps at Pura Besakih and the rather aggressive hawkers – to avoid these, find a driver who will also act as your guide. This tour takes you from the Klungkung Regency into the Karangasem Regency; it won't involve too much driving if you are based in Ubud or Candidasa, and it can be combined (on separate days) with tours 2 (Ubud) or 7 (Ten-ganan, Candidasa and Amlapura).

Kambang rests on a giant stone 'turtle' that appears to float in the middle of a pond.

Further back is the **Kori Agung** (main gate) of the palace. Look for Chinese, Portuguese and Dutch fig-ures on it alongside demons and animals. The wooden doors, carved

Judgement Day
In the Kerta Gosa, the amazing ceiling murals in the *wayang* puppet style of Kamasan, repainted on asbestos panels several times since the 1920s, illustrate a story from the Indian *Mahabharata* epic, in which Bima Swarga fights in hell and heaven to recover and purify the souls of his father and stepmother. The panels beneath this depict the terrifying punishments that await sinners in hell. Criminals facing trial must have shivered before the judges as they contemplated the seriousness of their actions.

Food and Drink 🍴

① LERENG AGUNG RESTORAN
Desa Abuan, Karangasem; daily 10am–6pm; $$
Tour buses stop at this restaurant, where there is an astonishing view incorporating a patchwork of terraced rice fields, river valleys and the volcano. Guests are served an all-you-can-eat, fixed-price Indonesian buffet lunch.

② LIHAT SAWAH
Banjar Tebola, Sidemen, Karangasem; tel: 0366-530 0516/
530 0519; daily 7am–10pm; $–$$
This charming restaurant in the rice fields is part of a small and friendly, family-run guesthouse. Semi open-air, it offers spectacular views of the countryside. The menu includes simple Western dishes and Indonesian specialities.

Gunung Agung Eruption

In February 1963, during preparations for the Ekadasa Rudra sacrifice (held once a century), glowing clouds of ash belched from the Gunung Agung volcano. After lying dormant for 120 years, it erupted in March with such violence that the top 100m (330ft) were blown apart. The earth shook, putrid black smoke shot into the air, there were deafening explosions and blinding white flashes, and huge boulders were catapulted out of the centre. Over 1,600 people were killed in the eruption and a further 500 died in the aftermath. The population of the east of the island was threatened by toxic gases, molten lava and colossal rocks. Some 100,000 people were left homeless, and most lost their livelihoods, as entire villages were flattened. Built on a ridge, however, Pura Besakih suffered minor damage. Most Balinese viewed the eruption as punishment for performing the centennial ritual at the wrong time, while others saw it as a supernatural presence that needed to be appeased with human victims. In 1979, a correctly timed Ekadasa Rudra ceremony was held without incident.

with monkey brothers Sugriva and Vali from the Hindu *Ramayana* epic, were said to have shut by themselves after the *puputan (see p.53)*, and no one has been able or dared to open them since. The **museum** next to this displays temple artefacts, photographs, dance costumes and textiles from Klungkung.

Across the street is the towering black **Puputan Klungkung Monument** that commemorates the *puputan*.

PURA BESAKIH

From the main crossroads at Klungkung, head north 21km (13 miles) to **Pura Besakih ❷** (daily 7am–6pm; charge, plus extra charge for cameras), known as the 'Mother Temple'. This is the largest and most important temple complex on the island, situated on the slopes of the 3,142m (10,300ft) **Gunung Agung** *(see feature, left)*. The temple is believed to date to the 14th century and is actually a complex comprising 22 temples resting on parallel ridges. Stepped terraces and stairways ascend to a number of courtyards and gateways, leading up to the main temple building.

Pura Penataran Agung Besakih

The most important temple here is **Pura Penataran Agung Besakih** with its many multi-roofed *meru* (pagodas). Only worshippers may enter, but visitors can circle the outer walls to glimpse inside and for spectacular

views beyond (check out the view from the northeastern end).

Inside the main courtyard are three thrones rising from a single base for the three forms of Shiva, the destroyer. Two other temples symbolise the Hindu trinity: Pura Kiduling Kreteg (Temple South of the Bridge) for Brahma, the creator, and Pura Batu Madeg (Temple of the Upright Stone) for Vishnu, the preserver.

MUNCAN

There are several small restaurants in the car park, but the food there is mediocre, so return to the main road instead and drive 2km (1¼ miles) south to **Rendang**. Turn left on a road leading 4km (2½ miles) east to the old-fashioned village of **Muncan ❸**, alongside the fast-flowing, sacred Telaga Waja River, where monkeys can be seen playing in the trees, and the local farmers grow *salak* (snakefruit). Take time to marvel at the spectacular rice terraces, carved into the mountain sides. Further along the road you will see the sign to **Lereng Agung**, see ⑪①, on the left-hand side.

SIDEMEN

Continue east through Selat, turning right before Duda and then south 10km (6 miles) to the rural, scenic **Sidemen ❹**, which for generations has produced masters of Balinese literature and Hindu theology. The village is also famous for its hand-woven textiles. You can watch the weavers at work on their wooden hand-operated looms. You may consider staying at this village; if you do, a nice spot for dinner is **Lihat Sawah**, (meaning 'rice field view'), see ⑪②.

Alternatively, continue downhill for about 6km (4 miles) until you reach the junction at the main road. From here you can turn right in the direction of Ubud, or left towards Candidasa.

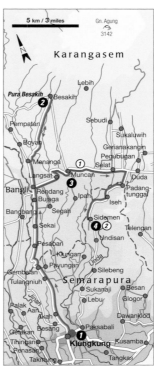

Above from far left: Pura Besakih; women weaving double *ikat* cloth, Sidemen; Pura Penataran Agung Besakih.

Holy Mountain

The Balinese treat Gunung Agung, Bali's highest and holiest mountain, with the greatest respect. They sleep with their heads facing it and spend a great part of each day pacifying, worshipping and entertaining the gods who are believed to live there. The water from its sacred springs is also highly sought after for temple rites.

TENGANAN, CANDIDASA AND AMLAPURA

In the royal Balinese regency of Karangasem, visit an ancient walled stronghold famous its textiles and bloody ritual battles. Drop by a former palace, wander through a water palace and travel through the mountains past traditional villages.

DISTANCE 58km (36 miles)
TIME A full day
START/END Candidasa
POINTS TO NOTE

A car, either self-drive or ideally with a driver, is essential for this trip. There is nothing strenuous about it, and it's a fun day out for children with lots of fascinating activities at Tenganan, including watching the gentle buffaloes that wander through the village streets. Later in the day, kids will find plenty of space to run around at Taman Ujung. Bring some cash, because Tenganan is good for handicrafts – don't forget to barter *(see p.19)*. This tour is perfect if you are based in Candidasa, and follows on well (on separate days) from tour 6 of Klungkung and Besakih *(see p.53)*.

Water Sports Off Candidasa

There are several superb snorkelling and dive sites off Candidasa; ask at any of the beach-front hotels, where you can arrange to be taken in a traditional *jukung* fishing boat to Tepekong Island and the tiny tree rock Mimpang Islands off the coast. There are several coral walls here where you will see a plentiful variety of marine life, including sponges, nudibranch and other small creatures. In the open waters you may even spot sharks and manta rays.

The island's magnificent eastern regency of Karangasem is an exotic Balinese kingdom of forests and mighty mountains, emerald rice ter-races, ancient temples, mystical water palaces and quiet beaches.

Named after an old temple on a nearby hillside, **Candidasa ①** is a peaceful seaside destination and a great base from which to visit the regency's many attractions. Notable features include the sacred lotus lagoon just beside the beach and a number of off-shore islets and coral reefs, which make for ideal diving and snorkelling *(see margin, left)*. There are numerous hotels and restaurants here.

TENGANAN

After an early breakfast, drive just to the west of Candidasa to a turn-off that heads about 4km (2½ miles) north (inland) to **Tenganan ②**, a 700-year-old walled village hidden in the hills (daily 7am–6pm; charge). After signing the visitors' book and paying a small fee at the booth, you enter the village to see stone ramps on three broad parallel avenues running north to south, with narrow lanes running east to west and forming a grid.

Tenganan is one of Bali's original pre-Hindu settlements and a stronghold of native traditions. The residents are the Bali Aga people, descendants of the aboriginal Balinese who resisted the rule of the post-Majapahit kings, fiercely safeguarding and maintaining their own culture through the conviction that they were descended from the gods. They practise a time-honoured lifestyle based around ritual and ceremony, bound by strict *adat* (customary law) practices to maintain purity.

Council of Elders

The buildings in the village have been meticulously positioned in accordance with long-established beliefs. Walking through the village you will see some ceremonial longhouses on your left in the middle of the west lane, including the imposing Bale Agung, where the council of elders makes its decisions. The walled house compounds of the purest descendants line the two sides of this lane, while the east lane is for villagers who have married anyone from the outside.

Living Museum

This fortress-like village has become a living museum, and, as you stroll through the avenues past docile buffaloes with their calves, the villagers may invite you into their houses. These also function as shops and workshops, where expert craftsmen and women carry out centuries' old skills, including the inscription and decoration of *lontar* palm books, which you will see at the southern end of the village – do ask for a demonstration. *Ata* vine basketry is typical of Tenganan, and you will see the baskets woven from this strong vine laid out in the sun to dry at the northern end of the village. The people tend to be friendly and won't hassle you to buy their products.

Shimmering Cloths

Tenganan is the only place in Indonesia where the double-*ikat* cloth, known as *kain geringsing,* is made. Villagers believe that Indra, the Hindu lord of storms, created and taught the people of Tenganan how to weave these textiles. Undyed threads for both weft and warp directions are wound on two separate frames that are the exact length and width of the finished cloth. Charcoal grids are marked on them, and waterproof fibres are tied in complex patterns. The threads are then coloured with

Above from far left: lotus at Candidasa; a Bali Aga woman prepares for a festival at Tenganan.

Pasir Putih Beach

The most beautiful beach on the coastline is Pasir Putih, meaning 'white sands', situated 6km (4 miles) east of Candidasa. Fringed by a coconut grove and flanked by green headlands with a sheer cliff behind, it is accessed by a 600m/yd track, which, although rough and steep, is negotiable by car. The tranquil ambience and the peppering of simple grass-roofed *warungs* (cafés) are reminiscent of the Bali of the 1970s.

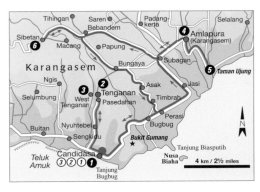

natural dyes. This process may be repeated several times, with new sections tied off, while others are opened up. Finally, all the fibres are removed, and the threads are woven. The dyed sections overlap precisely to form exquisite designs. This difficult and time-consuming technique – it can take up to seven years to produce a single piece – is otherwise used only in a few villages in India and Japan. The weavers strap themselves into small looms, leaning backwards and forwards to adjust the tension of the threads with their bodies, nudging the threads into position with a pointed twig. The ritually significant cloth is believed to have the power to protect the wearer from sickness and evil. The name may come from the words *gering* (ill) and *sing* (not), although *geringsing* itself means 'speckled', an appropriate description of this shimmering textile.

Bloody Ritual Battles

The ritual *mekare-kare* is staged annually in Tenganan in June or July as part of the Usaba Sambah festival. Each duel, which involves the young men of the village fighting each other with prickly *pandanus* leaf whips, takes place to the intense martial sounds of the *gamelan selonding* and lasts only a few seconds, accompanied by much merriment and laughter. The attacks are warded off with tightly woven *ata* vine shields; there are no winners and no losers, because the objective is to draw blood as an offering to the gods. After the battles, the combatants' wounds are treated with a stinging mixture of alcohol and turmeric, leaving no scars.

On the first day of the *mekare-kare* the unmarried maidens of the village ride on creaky wooden ferris wheels, which are manually operated by the men. The turning is supposed to symbolise the descent of the sun to the earth.

Village Customs

The Bali Aga society is communal, with a distinct social organisation. All of the village property and surrounding fertile farmland belongs to the township as a whole. The villagers do not actually work the land; instead they lease it to sharecroppers from other villages and receive half the harvest. This leaves the Tenganese free to engage in artistic activities such as weaving, dancing and the music of the *gamelan selonding* (an iron-keyed metallophone), an ancient version of the *gamelan*. They also faithfully adhere to a calendar of complex ceremonies and ritual trance fighting, known as *perang padan* or *mekare-kare*, using prickly *pandanus* leaf whips to draw blood *(see box, left)*.

WEST TENGANAN

If you have time, stop at **West Tenganan** ❸ – you will see the turning signposted on the right-hand side as you drive back to the main road. This village was once part of the original Tenganan but separated by a river after a flood. Quieter and much less visited than its eastern counterpart, West Tenganan is similar but not bound by such strict *adat* (customary law) practices. Here, you can also enter villagers' houses, buy handicrafts and watch artisans at work creating *lontar* palm books, making baskets and weaving textiles.

AMLAPURA

Drive back to the main road and stop for an early lunch in Candidasa – Vincent's, see ⑪①, is a popular place.

After lunch, continue 20km (12 miles) east over the hills and into **Amlapura** ❹, the largest town in East Bali and the capital of the Karangasem Regency. In fact, it used to share the same name as the regency, but, in 1963, after the catastrophic eruption of Gunung Agung, the town was 'reborn' as Amlapura to rid itself of any fateful association that villagers were concerned might provoke a much-dreaded recurrence.

Puri Agung Karangasem

The main attraction of Amlapura is the *puri*, or palace, Puri Agung Karangasem.

There is a western, a northern, a southern and an eastern *puri*; of these, only the **Puri Kanginan** (Eastern Palace; daily 9am–5pm; charge), on the main road to the market, is easily visited. Follow the one-way streets all around the edge of town until you see it on your left.

Enter the front courtyard of the palace to see the Bale Kambang (Floating Pavilion), set in the middle of a large pond. The pavilion was once used by the royal family for relaxation and entertainment.

Located nearby is the European-style Bale Maskerdam, or 'Amsterdam Hall', inside which are housed old photographs, sedan chairs and other royal artefacts. The Maskerdam faces the Bale Pemandesan, or tooth-filing pavilion, which showcases decorative carvings of flowers and animals, executed during the 1920s by Chinese craftsmen.

Above from far left: the lagoon at Candidasa; the community at Candidasa; puppet for sale in Tenganan walled village.

Last Raja of Karangasem
The last raja of Karangasem was Anak Agung Anglurah Ketut Karangasem (1887–1966), who, in 1908, succeeded his uncle as *stedehouder* or local ruler under the Dutch colonial system. A born architect and lecturer, he built three water gardens and wrote many philosophical, ethical and religious notes, hymns and poems in the Indonesian and Balinese languages. He also had 12 wives and 32 children.

Above from left:
Taman Ujung; Pura
Ulun Danu Bratan.

Above: walkway
detail and statue of
the Ganges river god-
dess Dewi Gangga at
Taman Ujung.

TAMAN UJUNG

From the centre of Amlapura near the market, head 4km (2½ miles) south to reach **Taman Ujung** ❺ (daily 8am–6pm; charge). This picturesque pleasure park and water garden was built in 1919 by the last raja of Karangasem, Anak Agung Anglurah Ketut Karangasem *(see margin, p.59)*. The water palace was formally used from 1921 as a place for the raja to entertain honourable dignitaries, as well as being a retreat for the royal family. It had a vast pool bordered by small pavilions and a European building with stained-glass windows in the centre. Most of the park was destroyed by the 1963 volcanic eruption of Gunung Agung *(see p.54)*, but in 2004 it was completely restored to its former glory. It is a great place for escaping from the heat.

Food and Drink

② **TOKE**
Jl Raya Candidasa; tel: 0363-41991; daily 10.30am–late; $$
At this luxuriously decorated restaurant, tables spill out into a candlelit garden. The menu is a range of Western, Balinese and Indian food, with lots of seafood and a blackboard of daily specials.

③ **WATERGARDEN KAFE**
Jl Raya Candidasa; tel: 0363-41540; www.watergarden hotel.com; daily 7am–10.30 pm; $$$
The food is reliably good at the romantic, open-air Watergarden Kafe hotel restaurant. The extensive, eclectic menu offers Asian and European cuisine as well as fresh seafood, with classic dishes from Vietnam, Japan, China, Thailand, Morocco and Germany.

SCENIC VILLAGES

Backtrack to Amlapura and head 2km (1¼ miles) west, taking a small turn-off road, leading 9km (5½ miles) uphill through **Bebandem** and over to **Sibetan** ❻. The road sides are lined with short, thorny trees, which produce *salak*; if in season, buy this fruit with its brown, scaly, snake-like skin and crisp, sweet-tart flesh.

Return to Bebandem and take the road to your right going 8km (5 miles) downhill through the Bali Aga villages of **Bungaya**, **Asak** and **Timbrah**, which are in many ways similar to Tenganan, although not quite as extraordinary. Perpendicular to the main road, note the narrow village lanes that allow only two people to pass. Long ceremonial pavilions are the focus of attention for Usaba Sambah rituals held in the villages during June, July and August. These feature dances and battles to honour the Dewi Sri, the rice goddess, and Rambut Sedana, the god of prosperity.

The road joins the main coastal road, so turn right and head 6km (4 miles) west back over the hills to Candidasa. Along the way, pause at a small pavilion along the road side to admire the stunning rice fields. There are plenty of dining options in Candidasa: you might want to check out **Toke**, see ②, a popular restaurant with the same owners as Vincent's *(see p.59)*; or the romantic **Watergarden**, see ⑪③.

BRATAN AND BEDUGUL

This action-packed tour takes in a market, a lakeside temple and some beautiful botanical gardens. It's a fun trip for kids, as they will have a chance to swing through the tree tops or jet-ski on the lake.

Bali's lake district, set within the vast crater of an ancient, extinct volcano, offers numerous attractions. The refreshing temperature at this high altitude is an average of 10ºC (50ºF) below the coastal regions, and the views are magnificent, extending across three lakes towards dense rain-forests and angular mountains. Make an early start after breakfast, as this is a full day tour.

LAKE BRATAN

Lake Bratan is surrounded by magnificent scenery, with the 2,020m (6,627ft) Gunung Bratan the most prominent feature. The area round the lake is well equipped to cater for visitors.

Candikuning Market

Start the day at **Candikuning ❶**, the main village in the lakeside resort area known as Bedugul, where there are several hotels. Begin by visiting the daily **Bukit Mungsu Market**, a riot of colour and activity. Nowadays, it caters largely for visitors, selling handicrafts and souvenirs such as woodcarvings, but it will also give you an insight into some of the locally grown flowers,

DISTANCE 26 km (16 miles)
TIME A full day
START Candikuning
END Munduk
POINTS TO NOTE
This tour offers a great day out for families; kids will love posing for photographs with the animals, as well as the strawberry treats, the water sports and Treetop Adventure Park. Note that the day does include some strenuous activities, but all of these are optional. A car, either self-drive or, ideally, with a driver, is essential. While it is possible to get to Bedugul by shuttle bus, with services operating daily from Kuta/Sanur/Ubud, there is only one drop-off point. Remember to bring swimming costumes, and if you plan to do a circuit at Treetop Adventure Park wear comfortable clothes and trainers. If you are coming from the south, travel north to Bedugul. The tour finishes at Munduk; from there you can continue northwest to the north coast road and Lovina to combine this tour with the next one *(see p.66).*

Balinese Markets

Food markets, characterised by strong aromas and lots of hustle and bustle, can be found all over the island. From as early as 4am, a bounty of fruit and vegetables including cauliflowers, avocados, bananas, pineapples, lemon-grass, chillies, peanuts, shallots, mangosteen, rambutan and *salak* (snakefruit), is off-loaded from trucks and artistically arranged in crates, plastic bowls and buckets by the vendors.

Towering *Meru*
Bali's elaborately tiered temple shrines are known as *meru*, symbolising the world mountain, Gunung Maha Meru. Reminiscent of a Chinese pagoda, a *meru* is constructed of an odd number, up to 11, of thatched tiers. The laws of traditional Balinese architecture carefully specify the dimensions, the form of construction, the appropriate materials, and the ceremonies that are required for its dedication.

fruit, vegetables and spices. Make sure you seek out some of the beautiful orchids that are on sale here.

'Floating' Temple

Head down the hill, and the road will bring you alongside the picturesque, alpine-like, Lake Bratan. About 1km (½ mile) from the market, you will see the temple, **Pura Ulun Danu Bratan** ❷ (daily 8.30am– 6pm; charge), which appears to float on the surface of the water. You'll find images of this temple, often shrouded in mist, on every postcard rack in Kuta.

This large 17th-century Hindu-Buddhist temple complex is set within landscaped gardens. Two multiple-roofed *meru* (pagodas) sit at the edge of Danau Bratan and honour the lake goddess, Dewi Danu, who is the provider of irrigation water for rice fields in the form of bubbling natural springs. The pagodas are not completely surrounded by water, but connected to the shore by narrow

strips of land and bamboo bridges, which are erected at the time of temple festivals and ceremonies. A nearby *stupa* (memorial shrine) has four Buddhas in niches around its sides facing the four major compass points. Although entry to the temple itself is not allowed, the surrounding view of the temple complex, beautiful gardens and the majestic but often clouded Gunung Catur is definitely worth seeing. Here, you will see animal keepers, who will invite you to have your photograph taken with pythons, bats, iguanas, civet cats and hornbills.

Strawberry Stop

This cool mountainous area was a favourite place of escape from the heat and humidity for the Dutch colonialists. The climate is perfect for cultivating strawberries, so now might be a good time to taste some of this famous local produce. Take a break at **Strawberry Stop**, see ⑪①, 200m/yds north of the temple complex on the

opposite side of the main road, where you can enjoy strawberries galore, served in a variety of ways. You can even have a light lunch here, but for something more substantial you could try **Café Teras**, see ⑪②, just 1.5km (1 mile) further north. This will set you up for an active afternoon, with a choice of water sports on the lake, a tree-top adventure or a stroll through the botanical gardens.

Bedugul Recreation Park

If the water looks tempting, **Taman Rekreasi Bedugul** ❸ (Bedugul Recreation Park; daily 8am–6pm; charge), on the southern shores of Lake Bratan offers parasailing, speedboat rental, jet-skiing and water-skiing. Follow the road back up the hill past the market and continue for a further 2km (1¼ miles) until you reach the turning on the left, signposted 'Objek Wisata, Bedugul Water Sports'.

Botanical Gardens

Alternatively, to the west of the market are **Kebun Eka Raya Botanical Gardens** ❹ (Bedugul Botanical Gardens, Candikuning; tel: 0368-22050/21273; daily 8am–6pm; charge). Look out for the statue of the giant corn on the cob, immediately south of the market – the signpost to the gardens is at this junction.

The Botanical Gardens make up a cool, shady park covering 132 hectares (326 acres) of tropical rainforest on the slopes of Gunung Pohon (tree mountain), with over 650 different species of trees and nearly 500 varieties of wild and cultivated orchids; there is even a cactus hothouse. You won't feel as if you're in Bali while wandering around the clearly marked paths through tropical 'alpine' forests of pine trees. The clean, crisp air is very refreshing.

Treetop Adventure Park

The Botanical Gardens are also home to **Bali Treetop Adventure Park** ❺, (Bedugul Botanical Gardens, Can-

---

Food and Drink 🍴

① STRAWBERRY STOP

Jl Raya Denpasar-Singaraja, Bedugul; tel: 0362-21060; daily 8am–6pm; $

This simple restaurant is attached to a strawberry farm and serves its home-grown produce in a variety of ways: strawberries whipped into milk shakes, squeezed into juices or stuffed into pancakes with strawberry ice cream and strawberry wine. Also does light meals.

② CAFÉ TERAS

Jl Raya Denpasar-Singaraja, Lempuna, Bedugul; tel: 0362-29312; daily 7am–10pm; $$

A Japanese owned cottage restaurant with an air-conditioned colonial-styled dining room and a pretty garden terrace. Offers a menu of Japanese dishes including Miso soup, fusion pasta dishes, salads and teriyaki-style dishes as well as some Indonesian favourites. Alcoholic drinks include sake.

Above from far left: tempting fruit at market in Bedugul; shady canopy at the Botanical Gardens.

Magnificent Playground

Bali Handara Kosaido Country Club (tel: 0362-342 2646; www.balihandarakosaido.com), overlooking Lake Buyan, lays claim to being the only golf course in the world that is nestled inside the caldera of an ancient volcano. It is also listed among the world's top 50 most beautiful courses. The perfectly manicured fairways are complemented by colourful azalea, hibiscus and gladioli and lined by shady mature trees, with a dramatic backdrop of mountains, rainforest, and the peaceful lake.

Hydrangea Harvest

Balinese Hindus believe that their beautiful island is a gift, and for this they pay daily homage by leaving offerings on raised shrines for the attention of the gods and their ancestors, and on the ground to appease demons. These tiny woven palm-frond trays, lined with banana leaf and containing a symbolic assortment of rice, flower petals and incense, are known as *canang*, and the flower most commonly used in these offerings – and cultivated specifically for this purpose – is the blue hydrangea. Hydrangeas, or *pacah seribu*, are grown mainly in the mountainous regions of Bali. A visit to the fertile volcanic ridge above lakes Buyan and Tamblingan will reveal boundless fields of the sapphire-tinged flowers stretching to the sea.

dikuning; tel: 0361-852 0680; daily 8.30am–6pm, last admission 4pm; charge), where you and your children can venture from tree to tree through suspended bridges, spider nets, Tarzan jumps, flying swings and flying foxes. Complying with international safety standards, there are six circuits of varying levels to thrill everyone from small children to adrenaline junkies. Allow 2½ hours to complete the circuits; the Squirrel Circuits, for children aged 4–8, take 1½ hours to complete.

LAKE BUYAN AND LAKE TAMBLINGAN

If you want to explore the area a little further, there are some good places for overnight stays (see p.99). Otherwise, follow the main road northwest, up a long, steep winding hill – the walls of the ancient crater. Here, you'll see gregarious grey monkeys frolicking at the road side.

At the top of the hill, turn left along the crater rim road to the two smaller lakes: **Danau Buyan** ❻ (Lake Buyan) and **Danau Tamblingan** ❼ (Lake Tamblingan). These were a single body of water, until a landslide divided them in 1818. Motorboats and water sports are forbidden on these two lakes – the natural spring that feeds them provides water for drinking, and the lakes are also a rich source of fish, evident by curious wooden, offshore fishing platforms.

MUNDUK

Continue 6km (4 miles) to **Munduk** ❽, a clove- and coffee-growing village overlooking rice terraces, tobacco fields and orange groves. Nearly every gateway here is adorned with pink bougainvillea. Look out for the local people raking and sifting their coffee beans in courtyards beside the road.

Archaeological evidence indicates that a community was in existence in Munduk from between the 10th and 14th centuries until the Dutch took control of North Bali in the 1890s and turned this area into a cash crop-producing region. Stop for *pisang goreng* (banana fritters) and locally harvested coffee at **Ngiring Ngewedang**, see ⑪③, perched up above the road with spectacular views of palm trees, valleys and jungle stretching to the northwest coast and volcanoes of East Java.

Munduk Waterfall

Below the restaurant, 1km (½ mile) along the road, is the 246m (805ft) high **Munduk Waterfall** ❾ (charge). It is well signposted and accessed via steps and a rough, narrow track lined with sweet-smelling clove trees. After a 10-minute walk, you will reach the foot of these majestic falls. This is an alluring place, where you can bathe and absorb the invigorating energy emanating from the fierce cascading water.

The road continues another 16km (10 miles) to Mayong, where it meets the main road to the coast. Turn right and go 10km (6 miles) to Seririt, then turn right again and head 16km (10 miles) to Lovina, where you can base yourself for the night.

In the evening, you may wish to treat yourself by dining at **The Restaurant at Damai Villas**, see ⑪④), set on the mountain slopes outside of Lovina. Here, a gourmet chef whips up exciting dishes using organic ingredients.

Food and Drink 🍴

③ NGIRING NGEWEDANG
Munduk, North Bali;
www.ngiringngewedang.com;
daily 10am–4pm; $
Robusta and Arabica coffee beans from the neighbouring food forests are processed and sold at this enchanting, family-run hill-top restaurant and coffee house. Their delicious simple local cuisine includes what are reputedly the best fried noodles and banana fritters on the island.

④ THE RESTAURANT AT DAMAI VILLAS
Jl Damai, Kayu Putih, Lovina; tel: 0362-41008; www.damai.com; daily 11am–3pm, 7–10pm; $$$$
This celebrated restaurant is located in a boutique retreat nestled on the side of a mountain with views extending to the ocean. Balinese classics are given a gourmet twist, utilising organic produce from the small on-site farm, combined with fresh seafood and imported delicacies. Be sure to make a reservation.

Above from far left: at the Botanical Gardens; Danau Buyan (left) is separated by a strip of land from Danau Tamblingan (right); Munduk Waterfall.

Rainforest Trek
You can trek through the rainforest between Lake Buyan and Lake Tamblingan, an area abundant in birdlife, where you may spot babblers, woodpeckers, ground thrushes and malkohas. On the road above this shoulder of land is a temple and a sign to Pura Ulun Danu Tamblingan, directing you 400m/yds down a meandering flight of steps to another temple beside the lake's edge; this one has a multi-roofed *meru* (pagoda).

LOVINA AND SINGARAJA

This tour goes dolphin-watching, and explores Bali's old capital of Singaraja, calling in at the world's only library of 'lontar' manuscripts. It also visits a hillside Buddhist monastery, followed by a chance to relax at some traditional bathing pools fed by hot springs.

Love in a Name
Lovina was given its name in the 1960s by the last king of Buleleng, who purchased a small tract of land in Kaliasem and built the Tasik Madu (Sea of Honey) Hotel. It is possible that the name was chosen to signify the love in the hearts of the people, or it may refer to a pair of Santen trees that the king planted and which grew to embrace each other.

DISTANCE 47km (29 miles)
TIME A full day
START/END Lovina
POINTS TO NOTE
For this leisurely day tour, you should base yourself on the north coast, in Lovina (ideally in the village of Kalibukbuk), as it begins with a 5.45am pick-up from your hotel by your boat captain. The tour can be done in one day with a break in the middle to relax after the early start, or it can be cut into two half-day tours. Children will love the dolphin-watching trip and the traditional hot-spring bathing pools. Bring swimming costumes for these, but dress respectfully for the city tour of Singaraja and the Buddhist monastery. If time permits, the second half of this itinerary can be tagged on to tour 8 *(see p.61)*.

The peaceful atmosphere, calm seas and palm-fringed dark-sand beaches of north Bali have been attracting adventurous young travellers since the 1970s. This tour explores this lovely area.

LOVINA

Lovina ❶ – actually a long string of coastal villages (Pemaron, Tukad Mungga, Anturan, Kalibukbuk, Kaliasem and Temukus) to the west of **Singaraja** – is an excellent base for exploring the north coast, as there are lots of hotels and restaurants here. The liveliest village is **Kalibukbuk** ❷.

Dolphin Trips

Lovina Bay has a pretty black volcanic-sand beach fringed by coconut palms against a backdrop of hills; the sea here is great for swimming, and the reef offers good snorkelling. Lovina is famous for the spotted, spinner and bottlenose dolphins that gather and play in large schools within the bay; note the dolphin statue beside the beach. A memorable activity is to go on an early morning **dolphin-watching excursion** (daily 6am; charge). There's no need to look for a tour operator, as all the boats offer the same trip for the same price; you will need to make arrangements the night before at your hotel and be ready at 5.45am (the boatman may knock on

your door to wake you up) for the ride in a motorised traditional *jukung* fishing boat, to the area where dolphins swim. About 90 percent of trips have successful sightings.

Return to Kalibukbuk for breakfast. **Café Made**, see ①①, on a street lined with restaurants, is a good option.

SINGARAJA

After breakfast, head 10km (6 miles) east by car to **Singaraja** ❸ – the name means 'Lion King', commemorating a palace built in 1604 by Raja Panji Sakti. For hundreds of years Chinese, Indian and Arab traders brought their products, religion and culture through this trade port, which was Bali's capital from 1855 until the Dutch moved it south to Denpasar after defeating the royal families there in 1906.

The city still has some good examples of colonial architecture and is a major educational and cultural centre of present-day Bali. It has two university campuses and is well known for its silver crafts and hand-woven

Above: spotting a dolphin; boats on the shoreline at Lovina.

Food and Drink 🍴

① CAFÉ MADE

Jl Ketapang, Kalibukbuk; tel: 081-337-422247; daily 8am–11pm; $
Located at the beach end of Jl Ketapang, 500m/yds from the dolphin statue, Café Made is open at the front, with views over the street. Inside, there are colourful artworks on the walls. It serves sandwiches, snacks, international favourites, classic Balinese and Indonesian dishes and fresh fish.

songket textiles, incorporating gold and silver threads.

Gedong Kertya

Stop by **Gedong Kertya** ❹ (23 Jalan Veteran; tel: 0362-22645; Mon–Thur 8am–3.30pm, Fri 8am–1pm; free), at the southern end of town. This library was founded in 1928 by the ruler of Buleleng, I Gusti Putu Djlantik, and the resident (government official during Dutch rule) of Bali and Lombok , LJJ Caron, who recognised the need to collect, copy and preserve thousands of *lontar* manuscripts *(see box opposite)*.

The manuscripts cover subjects including astronomy, mysticism, ritual ceremonies, rules and regulations, religion, Balinese architecture, Balinese philosophy, genealogy, homeopathy, *usada* (medical manuscripts), history of the Hindu kingdom, folklore and black magic. Dried fan leaves from the rontal palm are inscribed with a pointed stylus and wiped with oily burnt macadamia nuts to make the lines visible. Many also have fine illustrations. Since these books tend to decay over time due to attack from insects, humidity and fungus, you may see a librarian making a new copy of an old work. The library also has a collection of old publications, while some manuscripts and ancient *prasati* inscriptions on copper plates are also on display in glass cases.

Located nearby is **Puri Sinar Nadi Putra** ❺, once a part of the former royal palace and now a centre for beautiful handwoven silk textiles.

Old Harbour

From here, head 3km (2 miles) by car down Jl Gajah Mada towards the old harbour. Most of the original structures on the waterfront were destroyed by high waves in the early 1990s, but there are still a few Dutch-style buildings and a Chinese *klenteng* (temple) by the shore. Visitors are not usually allowed inside, but you can peer through the gates at the interior walls that are covered with paintings of Buddhist deities and figures. The Chinese were once very active as traders in Singaraja, and there is still a high concentration of them living in the city.

Look out for the monument of a soldier bearing a flag, jutting out over the water's edge. This is **Yuddha Mandalatama** ❻, commemorating the

Food and Drink

② KAKATUA BAR & RESTAURANT
Jl Pantai Binaria, Kalibukbuk; tel: 0362-41344/41144; daily 8am–11pm; $
At Kakatua, two open-sided pavilions are linked by a fish pond and pots of flowering plants. The delicious hearty fare from the simple open kitchen ranges from pizza, pasta and cauliflower cheese to Indian curries, Mexican fare, Thai dishes and home-made puddings.

③ SEA BREEZE
Jl Bina Ria, Lovina; tel: 0362-41138; daily 8am–11pm; $
This beach-side restaurant offers great value for money, with a menu that features Indonesian and Western café-style food, including superb breakfasts, sandwiches, snacks, healthy salads, fresh seafood, tropical juices and tempting desserts.

Indonesian struggle for independence against the Dutch from 1945 to 1949.

Lunch in Lovina
At this point, head back to Lovina for lunch. There are lots of cheap and cheerful restaurants on the two parallel streets that run down to the beach in Kalibukbuk. Check out **Kakatua**, see ⑪②, which has a huge menu. After lunch, have a rest or else take a dip in the safe waters of Lovina Bay at Kalibukbuk Beach before heading west for the second part of this tour.

BRAHMA ARAMA VIHARA

From Lovina, drive 8km (5 miles) west along the main road. At Dencarik turn inland (south) 1.5km (1 mile) to **Banjar** and follow the sign to the **Brahma Arama Vihara** ❼ (tel: 0362-92954; daily 8am–6pm, closed 10 days in Apr and Sept; free), a monastery located 2km (1¼ miles) up a steep hillside. This striking modern Theravada Buddhist monastery was built by a Balinese Buddhist monk in 1971 to replace an older one founded in 1958. Inside is a gilded Thai Buddha. Dress respectfully, speak softly and remove your shoes before entering.

AIR PANAS HOT SPRINGS

For the final stage of the tour, follow the narrow road further to **Air Panas** ❽ (daily 9am–6pm; charge), a natural hot spring set in a pleasant landscaped environment. In 1985, the tepid 38˚C (100ºF) sulphuric waters, which are believed to cure skin ailments, were channelled to pour out of carved serpent spouts into a set of traditional bathing pools, one of which is fed by 3m (10ft) high spouts to give a pummelling massage. There are showers, toilets and changing rooms, so have a relaxing soak before heading back to Lovina. If you need a recommendation for dinner here, **Sea Breeze**, see ⑪③, is a good inexpensive option.

Lontar Palm Leaf Paper

Fan-shaped *rontal* palm leaves, ideally 25cm (10in) long, are collected and dried, and the ribs cut out. The leaves are then soaked to remove the chlorophyll, cleaned before being dried again, and steamed using boiling water mixed with *liligundi* leaves and *gambir* (uncaria), in order to give the *lontar* its delicate yellow-red colour. A slow-drying process in a damp place follows to prevent the leaves from wrinkling. As soon as they are pliant, the leaves are stacked, flattened with a press, then perforated in three places with a tool called a *cempurit*. Each leaf is then bound and screwed tightly. The edges are refined with a plane, and the tips are cut very precisely to make them even. *Kincu*, a sort of lipstick imported from China, or else paint, is used to colour the *lontar* réd, after which it is kept for six months before inscription.

10

KRAMBITAN, PUPUAN AND MEDEWI

Visit two palaces at a royal town before heading up into the mountains past clove and coffee plantations and rice terraces. Drive through a giant tree and watch the sunset from a remote surf beach on the splendid west-facing coast.

DISTANCE 86km (53 miles)
TIME A full day
START Krambitan
END Medewi
POINTS TO NOTE
This tour in the Tabanan Regency involves a lot of driving on mountain roads, so will be less tiring if you arrange for a car and driver rather than self-drive. It links well with tour 11 *(see p.73)*.

Once a powerful kingdom, the rural region of Tabanan now incorporates vast expanses of terraced rice fields, royal palaces and historically important villages that function as centres for traditional music and dance.

KRAMBITAN

This tour begins at the royal town of **Krambitan ❶**, which is 9km (5½ miles) southwest of the city of Tabanan. Krambitan has two palaces, belonging

The Tektekan

The *tektekan* is an exciting rendition of the Calonarang exorcist trance drama performed to the rhythmic beating of bamboo slit drums, which produce a 'tek' sound when struck. *Tektekan* was traditionally used to chase away malevolent spirits that were responsible for bringing disaster, such as drought or pestilence, to a village. Performances were believed to restore balance and ensure fertility.

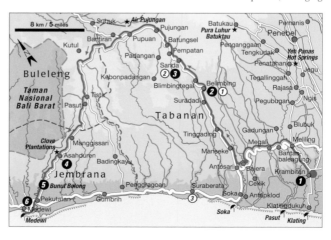

to a branch of the Tabanan royal family: the older **Puri Gede** and the newer **Puri Anyar**, (tel: 0361-812774; www.balipurikerambitan.web.id), both with beautiful architecture. The royal household here has a fine private collection of *lontar* manuscripts *(see p.69)*. Since 1972, 'Palace Nights' have been held for tourists at Pur Anyar. These involve a performance of the dramatic Calonarang trance play, known as a *tektekan (see margin, left)* by an ensemble from nearby Panarukan. Artists in Krambitan have also created a uniquely local style of *wayang* (puppet figure) painting – a traditional art in which the *wayang* puppet figures are depicted in paintings.

SCENIC DRIVE

From Krambitan, go northwest 5km (3 miles) back to the main road at Meliling. Turn left and drive 10km (6 miles) west to **Antosari**, then turn right and begin a scenic drive up the mountains towards Pupuan. There are two options for lunch en route; the first one is after about 12km (7 miles) at the village of **Belimbing ❷** (the name means starfruit). Here you will find the remote **Café Belimbing**, see ⑪①, set high above the road with spectacular panoramic views. Alternatively, continue another 9km (5½ miles) to **Sanda ❸** and stop for a feast at **Plantations**, see ⑪②, at Sanda Butik Villas. The awesome view from

this restaurant, which is located 700m (2,300ft) above sea level, takes in a vast wooded valley and rice terraces as far as the eye can see.

CLOVE PLANTATIONS

Continue north for another 8km (5 miles) to **Pupuan** and then turn left off the main road, heading first west and then south and downhill on a winding road. After 19km (12 miles) you will reach **Tista** (not to be confused with the trance dance village of Tista near Krambitan). Take the road signposted to **Asahduren ❹**, and 10km (6 miles) will bring you to the clove plantations – trim spice trees with orange tipped leaves. You might see and smell the fragrant flower buds drying on mats beside the road.

Above from far left: door detail, palace of Krambitan; Belimbing rice terraces.

Food and Drink 🍴

① CAFÉ BELIMBING (STARFRUIT CAFÉ)
Banjar Suradadi; daily 8am–9pm; no tel; $
This delightful, simple open-air café has panoramic views over rice terraces, coffee and clove plantations and an extensive menu as well as daily specials. The high-quality Indonesian and Western food includes healthy salads, snacks, pastas, wicked puddings and fresh fruit juices.

② PLANTATIONS
Sanda Butik Villas, Desa Sanda, Pupuan; tel: 0828-372 0055; www.sandavillas.com; daily 7am–9pm; $$
This open-air restaurant is set within the coffee-plantation grounds of a boutique hotel, offering glorious views over rice fields and a vast wooded valley. The extensive menu includes pasta, stir-fries, curries, Indonesian dishes and great salads using locally grown lettuces, asparagus, herbs and mushrooms. Also serves locally harvested coffee.

Above from left:
Medewi beach;
Pura Tanah Lot.

Banyan Trees
These trees continually sprout long aerial roots that grow down the trunk or dangle from a branch. Once these roots reach the ground and get a firm grip in the earth, they enlarge to form strong new trunks. The banyan is known as the 'tree that walks', because it moves forward – albeit slowly – with every new trunk that it puts out.

BUNUT BOLONG

From here, it's 11km (7 miles) down to the coast. Along the way, you will drive through **Bunut Bolong** ❺, a gigantic bunut, a type of banyan tree *(see margin, left)*, with the road going through a natural hole in its base. When the road was built, it was decided not to cut down such a huge tree, so the road went right through its trunk instead.

These massive banyan trees are a common sight in Bali – as you travel around, you will see them towering above almost every village temple and cemetery. Not only are they are considered to be the 'elders' of the tree kingdom, but it is believed that they are inhabited by spirits and demons, hence they are accorded special respect. They are carefully preserved and worshipped, and the Balinese build shrines at their feet, girding their trunks with the black-and-white chequered *poleng* cloth that marks the sacred. You may notice that motorists will honk their horns in polite greeting if they pass a banyan tree on the road. These majestic trees can grow to over 30m (100ft) in height and display a refreshing canopy of green above their multiple trunks.

A shrine guarded by colourful tiger figures has been built next to Bunut Bolong for the wayward local spirits to reside in. Just beyond the tree is a viewpoint with a splendid outlook over the expansive, forested mountains of western Bali.

MEDEWI

On the coastal route, continue 2km (1¼ miles) westwards to the dark-sand beach of **Medewi** ❻, where you can watch surfers catching the last breaks while the sun sets. It's not a good idea to swim here, though, as the waves can be huge, and the currents are very strong.

If you wish to spend some more time on this stretch of coast, take the main road east 16km (10 miles) to Balian – another popular surf spot named after the river estuary here – and stay at the enchanting **Gajah Mina Resort** on the headland. At the very least, why not have dinner at **Naga**, see ⑪③, the hotel's romantic restaurant, where you can sample delectable, healthy, fresh cuisine, much of it made with their home-grown produce.

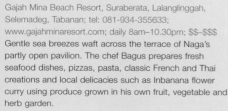

Food and Drink
③ NAGA RESTAURANT
Gajah Mina Beach Resort, Suraberata, Lalanglinggah, Selemadeg, Tabanan; tel: 081-934-355633; www.gajahminaresort.com; daily 8am–10.30pm; $$–$$$
Gentle sea breezes waft across the terrace of Naga's partly open pavilion. The chef Bagus prepares fresh seafood dishes, pizzas, pasta, classic French and Thai creations and local delicacies such as Inbanana flower curry using produce grown in his own fruit, vegetable and herb garden.

TANAH LOT, JATILUWIH AND BATUKAU

Begin with a Balinese blessing at a wave-lashed sea temple, then take in the magnificent views as you drive up the slopes of Gunung Batukau, Bali's second-highest peak, to a mountain temple. End at Yeh Panas hot springs.

The Tabanan Regency presents rice fields stretching from the coast up to an altitude of 700m (2,300ft). It is also home to Gunung Batukau, which, at 2,276m (7,467ft) above sea level, is the second-highest peak in Bali. It is known as the 'Stone Coconut Shell Mountain' thanks to its inverted *kau* or *karu* (coconut shell) profile.

Start early for this long, scenic trip. If you are staying in the south or the Ubud area, first drive to **Kerobokan** and then take the road 16km (10 miles) west to **Tanah Lot**, which is well signposted all the way. If you are staying in the Canggu area, you will see the signs on the main road directing you towards Tanah Lot. Visiting the temple of Pura Tanah Lot at this early hour means that you will be avoiding the bus loads of tourists that almost always arrive before sunset.

DISTANCE 73km (45 miles)
TIME A full day
START Pura Tanah Lot
END Yeh Panas
POINTS TO NOTE

This tour involves a lot of driving, so will be less tiring if you arrange for a car and driver rather than self-drive. Either way, opt for a four-wheel-drive vehicle with good brakes, as the roads are quite steep and twisting. Take extra caution during the rainy season (Nov–Mar). This tour is ideal if you are staying in the Seminyak or Canggu area. Alternatively, it can follow on from the Krambitan, Pupuan and Medewi route (see p.70), in which case it should be done in reverse. Don't forget to bring swimsuits with you.

Above: temple offerings at Pura Tanah Lot.

PURA TANAH LOT

Pura Tanah Lot ❶ (daily 7am–7pm; charge includes parking), the small 'Temple of the Land in the Sea', rests offshore on a rocky outcrop that becomes encircled by water at high tide. Scores of souvenir stalls line the pathway down to the beach, while rows of cafés occupy the cliff opposite the temple.

Pura Tanah Lot is one of the most important sea temples in Bali, and

Temple Festivals

Any visitor who spends more than a few days on Bali will be certain to see some kind of temple festival, colourful procession or ceremony. The *odilan*, or temple anniversary celebration, is a lavish ceremony commemorating the founding of a given temple. As the *odilan* date varies from one temple to another, you will probably have the opportunity to catch one at some point during your trip.

people from all over the island come here to pray, especially during the temple's *odilan* anniversary festival *(see margin, left)*. The temple was built in the 16th century by the legendary Hindu priest, Danghyang Nirartha, who left his home in Java as its population was converting to Islam. When he arrived in Bali, he is said to have fol-

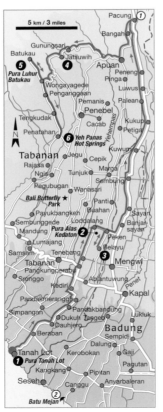

lowed a strange glow emanating from this spot, its natural beauty inspiring him to spend the night in meditation. When local inhabitants bothered him, he moved the land he was on out into the sea, thus giving it its name.

Holy Snakes

When Danghyang Nirartha departed, he instructed the people to build a temple here to commemorate his visit. He left behind his sash, which turned into poisonous sea snakes. These snakes are to be found living in caves and rocks around the base of the outcropping, and are said to guard the temple against intruders. You will be invited over to a cave on the mainland side to view (and even touch) one of these holy snakes, which will be coiled up asleep. In return for a nominal donation, the duty *pemanku* (lay priest) will illuminate the snake for you with his torch.

Hindu Blessing

At low tide, walk across the sand to a cave below the temple and receive a Balinese Hindu blessing from a priest in exchange for a donation. You will be asked to make a wish as you cup your hands and receive some holy water to ritually wash your face; the priest will then place some dried rice on your forehead – remember to leave this in place until it drops off. If this doesn't appeal, you can admire the view from the beach, watching the thundering waves crash behind the temple.

PURA ALAS KEDATON

Leave Tanah Lot and head inland (north) through **Beraban** on a road that winds 9km (5½ miles) through rice fields and small villages to **Kediri**. Drive north another 5km (3 miles) and turn right onto a road that takes you a short way east to **Pura Alas Kedaton ❷** (daily 7am–6pm; charge).

Known as the 'Temple of the Royal Forest', the temple complex has many monkeys and fruit bats living in the surrounding trees. The walk through the forest is more interesting than the renovated Pura Dalem, or 'Temple of the Dead', which you cannot enter. Guides will show you around for a small fee.

Backtrack to the main road and go 2km (1¼ miles) uphill before turning right at **Peken** and travelling the same distance south to **Belayu ❸**, where you can buy fine *songket* textiles, combined with gold thread and hand-woven by the village women.

PACUNG

Return to Peken and travel east for another 1km (½ mile) before turning left onto the very good paved main road leading 24km (15 miles) uphill to **Pacung**. Stop at **Pacung Indah Hotel**, see ⑪①, and enjoy a buffet lunch looking across magnificent rice terraces to the east, with the sacred mountain, Gunung Agung *(see p.54),* as a backdrop when the weather is clear.

JATILUWIH

The best is yet to come. Take the narrow winding road 13km (8 miles) west through steep rice terraces to **Jatiluwih ❹**, a Unesco World Heritage Site since 2008 for its preservation of traditional Balinese farming techniques. True to its name – 'extraordinary' or 'truly marvellous' – this scenic point at a height of 850m (2,700ft) above sea level offers one of the most breathtaking panoramic views imaginable, so take time to enjoy it. The rich pattern made by the banana plantations and the polka dots of newly planted rice are reminiscent of a complex batik. Your eyes will be led by steep-sided river valleys, dense forest and volcanic mountain crests.

PURA LUHUR BATUKAU

Continue along the road for 4km (2½ miles) to **Wongayagede**, and turn right on the main road for another

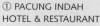

> **Food and Drink** 🍴
>
> ① **PACUNG INDAH HOTEL & RESTAURANT**
> Pacung; tel: 0368-21020;
> www.pacungbali.com;
> daily 8am–9pm; $–$$
> The restaurant at this hillside hotel, blessed with beautiful views, serves a daily Indonesian buffet lunch as well as *à la carte* meals. The focus is on local cuisine, but Western dishes are also available.

Agriculture and Fauna

The Tabanan Regency is known as Bali's 'rice bowl' and is the most agriculturally productive region on the island, yielding not only rice but also coffee, cacao, palm-sugar, vanilla, candlenut, cloves and tropical fruits such as durian, jackfruit, mangosteen, salak (snakefruit), coconuts and avocados. Meanwhile the area around Mt Batukau has the greatest biological diversity in Bali. Wildlife endemic to this area includes the small forest deer known as *kijang,* the rare, black leaf-eating monkey, the *landak* (porcupine), the *lubak* (mongoose), flying lizards and beautiful butterflies and moths.

Above from left: crossing the rice terraces near Jatiluwih; boats for seaweed cultivation, Nusa Lembongan.

2km (1¼ miles) to **Pura Luhur Batukau** ❺ (daily 8am–5pm; charge). This 'Lofty Stone Coconut Shell Temple' complex, which venerates the deities of mountains and lakes, is located about halfway up the mountain slopes of Gunung Batukau. It was the ancestral temple for the royal family of Tabanan, whose descendants still maintain the shrines today. Two smaller temples, Pura Dalem and Pura Panyaum, are found on the lower level. The main enclosure is at the higher mountain end, with several multiple-tiered *meru* (pagodas) for the deified kings.

On the eastern side is an artificial pond with two shrines in the middle. One is dedicated to the goddess of Danau Tamblingan *(see tour 8, p.64)*, while the other is for the god of Gunung Batukau, thus representing the concept of *rwa bhineda* (cosmic duality), the Balinese equivalent of Chinese yin-yang philosophy.

Below: a *canang sari*, or petal tray offering.

YEH PANAS HOT SPRINGS

Now descend 8km (5 miles) back down the main road to **Penatahan**, where you enjoy a soak in the sulphurous hot springs at **Yeh Panas** ❻ (daily 7am–7pm; tel: 0361-854 0851). Such natural phenomena as hot springs are believed in Bali to be frequented by spirits, and so Yeh Panas has a small temple, where people make offerings with prayers. The springs have been turned into a spa at a small resort, which non-residents may use for a fee; there are nine private and semi-private pools.

When you're finished, take the left turn-off going southeast for 4km (2½ miles), until it joins the main road heading 10km (6 miles) south through Wanasari and all the way down to Tabanan. From here it's an easy 13km (8 mile) drive to Sempidi, where major roads lead back to the main tourist centres. You may want to stop for dinner at **The Beach House**, see ⑪②.

Food and Drink

② THE BEACH HOUSE
Jl Pura Batu Mejan (Echo Beach), Canggu; tel: 0361-738471; daily 8am–11pm; $$
This popular restaurant has tables spilling out onto a beach-side bluff – a great place to watch the sunset. The international menu includes Indonesian dishes, and there is a daily barbecue of seafood. Friendly staff, potent Martinis and live music on Sunday evenings.

NUSA LEMBONGAN, NUSA CENINGAN AND NUSA PENIDA

Make a getaway to three nearby islands for water sports and time out on the beach. Explore the mangrove forest in a canoe, visit an underground cave house, then head for a temple associated with black magic.

Nusa Lembongan, the tiny, sparsely populated **Nusa Ceningan** and **Nusa Penida** are a trio of islands located 20km (12 miles) off Bali's east coast – just 30 to 60 minutes' cruise by boat from **Benoa Harbour**. Steeped in tradition, village life on Nusa Lembongan is slow and enchanting, and this is where most of the pleasure boats take visitors on packaged day tours. If you want to stay for a few days, there are alternative options for independent travellers.

NUSA LEMBONGAN

Arriving at **Nusa Lembongan ❶**, boats dock at Mushroom Bay and Jungut Batu. Despite its tiny size, the island offers lots of activities ranging from fishing, kayaking, diving and surfing to cycling, visiting the seaweed farms *(see margin, p.80)*, or exploring the mangrove forest in a dugout canoe. There are plenty of water-sport facilities, while restaurants range from barefoot beach bars to fine dining at **Jojo's Restaurant**, see ⑪① *(p.78)*.

DISTANCE On Nusa Lembongan and Nusa Ceningan 17km (10½ miles); on Nusa Penida 38km (23 miles)
TIME A day, or two days if you wish to visit Nusa Penida
START/END Nusa Lembongan
POINTS TO NOTE
If snorkelling and water sports are all you have in mind, book yourself on a day trip (Bali Hai Cruises; tel: 0361-720331; www.balihaicruises.com). These offshore islands are accessible on pleasure cruises or fast boats leaving Benoa Harbour, Serangan Harbour or Sanur (reliable operators are Blue Water Express, www.bwsbali.com, or Scoot Cruise, www.scootcruise.com). If you go by cheaper public boats, the crossing can be rough, slow, and even dangerous depending on sea conditions. You can also charter your own vessel, but this may end up riskier than a commercial cruise.

The majority of visitors swim, snorkel and nap for most of the day, as the weather can get very hot and dry. Crystal-clear waters in an idyllic bay make for excellent snorkelling and

scuba diving; the former from offshore pontoons or drifting charter boats, the latter with one of the PADI dive operators on the island, such as World Diving Lembongan (Pondok Baruna Guesthouse, Jungut Batu; tel: 081-239-00686; www.world-diving.com).

Dream Beach

If you're not into water sports, since the roads are generally well surfaced you could consider hiring a motorcycle (which any of the cafés at Mushroom Bay or Jungut Batu can arrange) and heading over to clearly signposted **Dream Beach**, on the south coast. The journey takes about 15 minutes. On the way, stop on the cliff top for a photo opportunity at **Devil's Tear ❷**, a rocky outcrop where the dramatic crashing of waves at full power creates water plumes and high-pressure spouts. Just south of here is Dream Beach, a gorgeous spot with an often-deserted beach of powdery white sand. Swimming can be dangerous though, as the waves are big, and the current can be very strong. Try **Café Pandan** at Dream Beach Huts, see 🍴②, for a casual lunch.

Jungut Batu

Alternatively, if time allows, a 30-minute or so walk from Mushroom Bay takes you to the main village of **Jungut Batu ❸**, with its sandy compounds and squat pavilions surrounded by thick and low coral or limestone walls. From here, take the beach road north and turn into the

Oceanic Sunfish

The channel between Nusa Lembongan and Nusa Penida is a renowned breeding ground for the Mola mola, or oceanic sunfish, a mysterious large, flattened fish with elongated dorsal and ventral fins, and a lumpy growth instead of a tail fin. It is the world's heaviest-known bony fish, with an average adult weight of 1,000kg (2,200lb). Divers come from all over the globe to witness this marvel, which can be seen from July to November.

Food and Drink 🍴

① JOJO'S RESTAURANT
Nusa Lembongan Resort Mushroom Bay, Nusa Lembongan; tel: 0361-725864; www.nusalembonganresort.com; daily 7am–10pm; $$$–$$$$
This upmarket resort restaurant is an open pavilion idyllically positioned to overlook the beach edging the coral bay. The menu offers a wide selection of Indonesian and international dishes, including plenty of fresh seafood.

② CAFÉ PANDAN
Dream Beach Huts, Nusa Lembongan; www.dreambeach lembongan.com; tel: 081-338-737344; daily 7am–10pm; $–$$
This open-air café and bar overlooks the stunning Dream Beach and offers a great selection of Balinese and Western dishes as well as a huge list of cocktails, which can be consumed in the café or on sunbeds on the sand.

③ MANGROVE RESTAURANT
Mangrove Point, Nusa Lembongan; daily 11am–9pm; $–$$
This rustic Robinson Crusoe-style restaurant is both romantic and close to nature. Set within the cool shady mangroves, it serves lots of classic Indonesian delights as well as a selection of simple Western dishes.

mangroves. Continue for 1½km (1 mile) to the Robinson Crusoe-style **Mangrove Restaurant**, see ⓕⓧ③, positioned at the eastern end of the spit of land that runs through the northern mangrove forest. You can also get there by boat from Mushroom Bay – any boat captain will know the way – or once there go on a delightful gondola-type boat ride through the shady mangroves. Be sure to bargain hard for a reasonable price, say Rp60,000, before you set out.

Continue on foot 1km (½ mile) further south to **Lembongan ❹**, a fishing village where the local people farm seaweed within a patchwork of underwater, bamboo-fenced plots. Along the way, pause on the hilltop where, on a clear

day, there are stunning views across Badung Strait to Bali. Birdwatchers should look out for flashes of white and turquoise denoting the sacred kingfisher (like the collared kingfisher but slightly smaller and common to this island).

Rumah di Bawah Tanah

At Jungut Batu on the south side of the hill, visit the cave house known as **Rumah di Bawah Tanah** (donation), a bizarre underground house built over 50 years ago by a local priest acting on divine inspiration. The multiple tunnels, nooks and crannies carved out from limestone can be rather eerie. Be sure to leave a donation to the late priest's family if you visit this oddity.

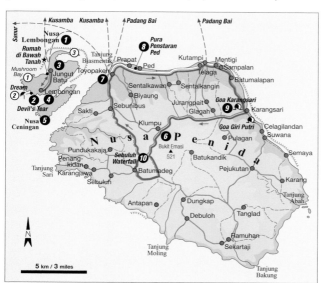

Above: Crystal Bay, on Nusa Penida; transporting seaweed on Nusa Penida.

Seaweed Harvest
Seaweed farming on the three islands is labour intensive and time consuming. Women are the main labourers, and growth is so fast that new shoots can be harvested every 45 days. The produce is then dried and exported, mainly to Japan, for processing and use in cosmetics. Most of Bali Hai's day cruises include a tour of the seaweed farm and village on Nusa Ceningan *(see p.77 for Bali Hai details)*.

NUSA CENINGAN

Later, follow the coast from the end of Jungut Batu beach, past Mushroom Bay to the Ceningan Strait on the east side of the island. This is a 3km (2-mile) walk. Alternatively, if you have hired a motorcycle, just follow the main road from the cave house in order to then cross on foot to the tiniest of the three islands, **Nusa Ceningan** ❺ (the name means small island) by means of a scenic suspension bridge. Crossing this quirky yellow bridge is an Indiana Jones experience; it feels a bit scary, as it rattles and swings, but it is safe. The island is home to a small village of seaweed farmers, whose boats you will see crowded around their plantations, like a floating marketplace, in the late afternoons. Return to your lodgings or boat before sunset as the paths are not lit at night.

NUSA PENIDA

If you are staying overnight on Nusa Lembongan, charter a boat (from Mushroom Bay or Jungut Batu) to take you early next morning to Toyopakeh, on the island of **Nusa Penida** ❻. This is the largest of the three islands, measuring approximately 200 sq km (77 sq miles), with towering limestone sea cliffs. There is little infrastructure and not many facilities for tourists, just a few *losmen* (family-run guesthouses) and a number of small *warungs* (road-side cafés/eateries).

During the 18th and 19th centuries, Nusa Penida was a penal colony for the Klungkung Kingdom, which meant that criminals, undesirables and political agitators were sent here after having been judged in the Kerta Gosa *(see p.53)*. In spite of these dubious roots, the people are quite friendly and welcome visitors to their remote 'Limestone Island'. Nusa Penida is famous for its *kain cepuk*, a handwoven *ikat* (weft tie-dyed) cloth with complex, multicoloured geometric patterns on a red or maroon background. Powerful magical properties are attributed to this textile, which is worn by Rangda, the widow-witch of Balinese exorcist drama.

Life is hard on Nusa Penida, with the locals making a living from fishing and farming, with seaweed probably the largest export. Few opportunities exist for education and employment.

Pura Dalem Ped

Settlers from Java, Lombok and Sulawesi are also to be found in the main town of **Toyopakeh** ❼. Pack lunch or snacks and lots of bottled water, then hire a vehicle with a driver for the day to first take you 3km (2 miles) east to the **Penataran Ped** complex and **Pura** ❽ (donation), the most important temple in the Bali Province for practitioners of black magic. Worshippers from all over Bali come here to pray during its *odilan*, or temple anniversary festival, which occurs once every 210 days. Everything is decorated with

Above from far left:
sifting through sea-
shells; Crystal Bay on
Nusa Penida; sea-
weed cultivation in
Toyopakeh harbour.

poleng (black-and-white chequered cloths), symbolic of negative and positive cosmic forces.

Always ask permission from the priests before entering, and don't forget to leave a small donation. Growing inside is a strange tangle of three different trees forming a great twisted mass and the atmosphere is rather spooky – as befits the temple's reputation. The patron deity here is Ratu Gede Mas Mecaling, the 'Fanged Lord of Victims', who, along with his invisible henchmen in the guise of fireballs, flies to Bali, landing on the beach at Lebih to spread disease and pestilence during the rainy season. The Balinese repel them with the lord's own fearsome image in the *barong landung* (tall puppet figures) of Jero Gede and his wife, Jero Luh, with their smiling faces.

Several other places on the island are worth visiting. Drive 10km (6 miles) along the northeast coast to see the enormous limestone cavern of **Goa Karangsari ❾**, with two shrines set in a grotto. The entrance lies 150m (492ft) up a steep stairway. Some of the branch tunnels lead to openings from where there are breathtaking views.

Continue south up into the hills, then northwest for 16km (10 miles) to **Sebuluh Waterfall ❿** near **Batu-madeg**, an unusual sight in such a dry place but really only impressive during the rainy season. Finally, head north, back to Toyapakeh before sunset for a boat to Lembongan, or return to Bali.

Below: Pura Segara,
dedicated to the sea
deity and part of the
Penataran Ped
temple complex.

DIRECTORY

A user-friendly alphabetical listing of practical information, plus hand-picked hotels and restaurants, clearly organised by area, to suit all budgets and tastes. Select nightlife listings are also included here.

A

ADDRESSES

Street names can be a cause of confusion in Bali, because many have been renamed due to historical or political figures falling in and out of fashion. In many cases a street is still referred to by its old name, but the signpost will show the new version. Additionally, in tourist areas it is not uncommon for a street to have a western 'nickname' (eg Double Six Street), taken from a long-established restaurant or club that perhaps dominates the street.

Note that 'Jl' stands for *Jalan*, which means 'Street'.

AGE RESTRICTIONS

In Bali and Indonesia the age of consent for heterosexual sexual activity is 19 years for males and 16 years for females. The age of consent for homosexuals is 18. The legal age for drinking is 18.

B

BUDGETING

Some average costs: a beer Rp 15,000; glass of house wine Rp 45,000 (local) or Rp 100,000 (imported); a main course at a budget restaurant Rp 15,000, moderate restaurant Rp 70,000, expensive restaurant Rp 150,000–250,000; a cheap hotel US$10–50, moderate hotel US$60–200, deluxe hotel US$200–1,000. Taxi journey to/from the main airport Rp 35,000–335,000; single bus ticket Rp 100,000.

C

CHILDREN

Children are universally loved in Bali. Babysitters are available at major hotels, and many hotels and resorts offer children's activities, crèche facilities and children's clubs. Some of these facilities are free of charge to hotel guests, while other hotels charge a daily or hourly rate; ask when booking.

CLOTHING

Bring casual clothing of lightweight natural fabrics, such as cotton, which offer the best comfort in the heat and humidity. Bali has a thriving garment industry, and clothes are readily available. Sandals or footwear that can be slipped off easily are a good idea, especially if planning to visit mosques or homes – shoes are always removed before going into a house. You'll need a light jacket or sweater if you're planning to visit mountain spots, and for air-conditioned buildings or vehicles.

CRIME AND SAFETY

While personal safety is not a general problem in Bali, as with anywhere in

the world it is important to be vigilant with your belongings. Pickpockets, car break-ins and drive-by bag snatching seem to be the most common complaints. It is not recommended to walk alone along Kuta beach at night. To reduce your risk, take the same basic precautions you would if you were visiting a big city, for example.

All thefts should be reported immediately to the police, even though there is little chance of recovering stolen belongings. This applies especially to passports and other official documents. Without a police report, you will have difficulty obtaining new documents and leaving the country, or claiming on your insurance policy.

All narcotics are illegal in Indonesia. The use, sale or purchase of narcotics results in long prison terms – even death – and/or huge fines. Don't keep or carry packages for people you don't know.

CUSTOMS

In addition to your embarkation card, a customs declaration form must be completed before arrival.

Indonesian regulations strictly prohibit the entry of weapons, narcotics and pornography. Fresh fruits, plants, animal products and exposed films and videos may be checked or even confiscated. Photographic equipment, laptop computers and other electronics can be brought in provided that they are taken out on departure. A maximum of 1 litre of alcohol, 200 cigarettes or 50 cigars or 100 grams of tobacco and a reasonable amount of perfume may be brought in. There is no restriction either on the import or the export of foreign currencies and traveller's cheques. However, the import and export of Indonesian currency exceeding Rp 10 million is prohibited.

The export of antiques more than 50 years old is not permitted; neither can ivory, tortoiseshell or crocodile skin be taken out.

D

DISABLED TRAVELLERS

The Balinese believe that all physical and mental disabilities are punishments for improper behaviour in past lives. That said, people with physical disabilities are viewed with compassion. Generally, there is very little consciousness in Indonesia about the special needs of disabled people. Due to rough pavements, high kerbs, an abundance of steps and a lack of ramps, it is difficult to move around Bali in a wheelchair. However, you will never have problems finding people who are more than willing to help you. Do make sure your wheelchair is in good working order before you come to Bali, as you may find it hard to locate a repair shop.

Above from far left: loaded up with rice sacks, Ketewel; *kecak* dance performed at Pura Luhur Uluwatu.

Electricity
Indonesia (including Bali) uses the 220-volt system, 50 cycles and a round, two-pronged slim plug; adapters are readily available. Power failures are common, with a number of all-day scheduled power cuts, but most hotels and restaurants have back-up generators. Bathroom shaver plugs usually have a transformer switch.

Green Issues

Bali is suffering from acute ecological problems. The rapid and unrestrained tourist development of the island has had a massive impact on its natural environment, causing deterioration of the water quality, destruction of the coral reefs, the decline of water resources and the escalation of pollution. Hotels have been constructed without regard to the water supply and waste disposal capacity, and many commercial developments do not conform to provincial regulations regarding the protection and integrity of historical and sacred sites. Thankfully, a collective segment of Bali's hotels is setting an example through membership of Green Globe 21. There are also some recyclable-rubbish pick-up services from private households.

E

EMBASSIES AND CONSULATES

Australia and Canada

Jl Hayam Wuruk 88 B, Tanjung Bungkak, Denpasar; tel: 0361-241118; www.dfat.gov.au/bali.
Consular hours: Mon–Fri 8am–noon, 12.30–4pm.
Visa hours: Mon–Fri 8.30am–noon.

UK and Ireland

Jl Tirta Nadi 20, Sanur, Denpasar; tel: 0361-270601; e-mail: bcbali@dps.centrin.net.id.
Opening hours: Mon–Fri 8.30am–12.30pm.

US

Jl Hayam Wuruk No. 188, Denpasar; tel: 0361-233605; e-mail: amcobali@indosat.net.id.
Opening hours: Mon–Fri 8am–noon, 1–4.30pm.

EMERGENCIES

Bali has an Emergency Response Centre, so you just need to dial **112** to be put through to the communication centre that co-ordinates all of its emergency services. You can also call:
Ambulance **118**
Fire Department **113**
Police **110**
Search & Rescue **111/115/151**

ETIQUETTE

The Balinese are remarkably friendly and courteous, even with so many visitors to their tiny island. They are also conservative, for tradition is the backbone of their culture.

Shaking hands on introduction is usual nowadays for both men and women. However, using the left hand to give or to receive something is taboo (the left hand is for personal hygiene purposes and therefore considered unclean), as is pointing with the left hand. Never touch anyone, even a child, on the head; a person's head is considered to be the most sacred part of the body. Crooking a finger to call someone is impolite; instead, beckon to the person by waving the fingers together with the palm facing down. Anger is not openly displayed; therefore aggressive gestures and postures, such as standing with your hands on your hips when talking, are considered to be insulting. Avoid pointing with the index finger as this gesture may be taken as a physical challenge. It is also offensive to point with your toes (as when indicating an item displayed on the ground in the market) or sit with the soles of your feet pointing at other people; this is because the feet are considered to be the lowliest part of the body. When passing in front of an older person or high ranking person, especially if they are sitting down, bend your body slightly. It is polite to wait until you are given per-

Above from far left: participants in a temple festival, Besakih village; pool with a view at the Karma Kandara; purification ceremony on the beach.

mission to eat or drink. Gracious behaviour is much appreciated by the Indonesians and will produce better results than an angry outburst.

Menstruating women and anyone with a bleeding wound must not enter temples due to a general sanction against blood on holy ground. At temple festivals, photographs without flash are fine but never stand in front of a seated priest, as one's head should not be higher than that of a holy person.

H

HEALTH

International health certificates of vaccination against cholera and yellow fever are required only from travellers coming from infected areas. Typhoid and paratyphoid vaccinations are optional, as are Hepatitis A and B injections. Diphtheria and tetanus vaccinations are recommended. Check the following websites for updates:
• **World Health Organisation**
www.who.int/ith/
• **MD Travel Health**
www.mdtravelhealth.com

Malaria and Dengue Fever
Malaria is not a significant problem in Bali; however, dengue fever is. Dengue-carrying mosquitoes are distinguished by their black-and-white banded legs and by biting in the daytime. They hide in dark and dank places (eg bathrooms),

closets and curtains. Protect yourself with long sleeves and trousers or use insect repellent *(obat anti nyamuk)*. If you are sleeping alfresco or in a non-air-conditioned room, use a mosquito net.

Minor Ailments
Treat any cut or abrasion immediately, as it can easily become infected in the humid climate. Betadine, a powerful non-stinging, broad spectrum anti-septic, is available in solution or ointment at any *apotik* (pharmacy).

Sexually Transmitted Diseases
Gonorrhoea and herpes are on the increase in Indonesia, as are AIDS and HIV-related infections. Prostitutes are not given health check-ups, and the so-called Kuta Cowboys or local gigolos have multiple partners from all over the world. Condoms – Indonesian and imported brands – are available at pharmacies and drugstores.

Bali Belly
Many travellers get some form of Bali Belly at some point in their stay. Taking Lomotil and Imodium will stop the symptoms, but won't cure the infection. At the first sign of discomfort (diarrhoea and cramping), drink strong, hot tea and avoid all fruits and spicy foods. Charcoal tablets (Norit brand) will help alleviate the cramping. If you get a fever along with these symptoms, find a doctor who can prescribe antibiotics. Mineral replacement salts (Oralite

Gay and Lesbian Issues
Male homosexuality is tolerated to a certain degree in traditional Balinese society, but those involved are eventually expected to marry and have children. Flagrant displays of romance, both gay and straight, are considered very distasteful.

Internet Facilities
Internet cafés can be found all over the tourist areas of Bali; expect to pay Rp 200–500 per minute for access. At the better Internet centres, you can make use of a variety of computing services including burning CDs and downloading digital photos. Travellers with their own laptops can find wireless access at an increasing number of restaurants and cafés.

Left Luggage
The left-luggage room at the airport is just behind McDonald's at the international departure terminal.

brand) for dehydration should be available at every local pharmacy. Drink as much liquid as possible.

Water

Bottled mineral water is widely available. All other water, including that from wells and municipal supplies, *must* be brought to a rolling boil and kept there for 10 minutes to make it safe for consumption. Iodine (Globolien) and chlorine (Halazone) tablets may also be used to make water drinkable. Brushing your teeth with untreated water is usually safe if you do not swallow the water. Ice in eateries is generally safe, as it is manufactured at licensed factories – but it is sometimes dumped in front of the restaurant on the dirty pavement and then only lightly washed. If in doubt, only consume drinks in cans or bottles.

Fruit should be peeled before eating, and avoid eating raw vegetables except at better restaurants for tourists. Go easy on spicy food if you're not used to it. It is best not to take chances with street-food vendors, but if you are dead set on it then stick to those not serving meats unless your system is already well adjusted. Remember to wash your hands thoroughly with soap.

Hospitals and Clinics

Bali is getting better in terms of hygiene and medical facilities, but it still has a way to go. It is strongly recommended that you take out private health insurance before you visit. If you do need

hospital treatment, particularly in the case of a life-threatening emergency, get to Singapore if your insurance policy covers medical evacuations. If not, your consulate may be able to help.

If you are in the Kuta area, BIMC (Bali International Medical Centre) and SOS Medical Clinic are geared up for the needs of tourists. For minor problems, most villages have a small government public health clinic, called *puskesmas*, used by local people and very inexpensive. The luxury hotels also have on-call doctors and good clinics.

Many hospitals and clinics charge different rates for Indonesians and foreigners, so be sure to check the list of fees for services to avoid getting a nasty shock when presented with the bill.

• **Bali International Medical Centre (BIMC)**
Jl Bypass Ngurah Rai 100X, Simpang Siur, Kuta, tel: 0361-761263; www.bimc bali.com. Open 24 hours.
• **International SOS Clinic Bali (KLINIK SOS Medika)**
Jl Bypass Ngurah Rai 505X, Kuta. 24-Hour Alarm Centre: tel: 0361-710505. Clinic: tel: 0361-720100; www.sos-bali.com.

Pharmacies

If you take prescription drugs, bring a sufficient supply. Pharmacies (*apotik*) can often fill a prescription, but the dosage may not be quite the same as your doctor has prescribed. Pharmacies are widespread in the towns and tourist

areas. They sell a wide range of medicines, many of which you would need a prescription for back home. Not all the assistants speak English.

L

LANGUAGE

The Indonesian national tongue, Bahasa Indonesia, is spoken everywhere. For some useful words and phrases, see the inside back cover flap of this book and the pull-out map. Bali also has its own indigenous language, Bahasa Bali. English is spoken in the main tourist areas, and many local guides are trained in Japanese and European languages.

M

MEDIA

Most large hotels and department stores have small bookstores, usually filled with the same tourist publications, coffee-table books, novels and English-language newspapers. There are many newspaper boys on the street eager to sell you newspapers from Australia and elsewhere. Remember that prices are negotiable. Some local English-language newspapers are also printed daily, such as *The Jakarta Post*, *Herald Tribune* and *Asian Wall Street Journal*, available at all major hotels, most bookstores and the magazine kiosks in Sanur, Kuta,

Denpasar and Ubud. *Time*, *Newsweek* and *International Herald Tribune* are also available at these places. Several free tourism-oriented magazines, such as *Bali Now*, *Hello Bali* and *The Beat*, can be found at hotels, restaurants and visitor information centres. Periplus Publishers' bookstores are widely located and found in most of the malls, offering a good selection of books on travel, history, politics, Indonesia and culture.

MONEY

The Indonesian monetary unit is the rupiah (Rp). Coins are in Rp 100, 200, 500 and 1,000 denominations. Paper currency is printed for Rp 1,000, 2,000, 5,000, 10,000, 20,000, 50,000 and 100,000 notes. Be aware that there are several versions of the same denomination of note.

Change for high-value notes is often unavailable in smaller shops, stalls or taxis, so hang on to coins or paper currency of Rp 1,000 and below, especially when travelling in outlying areas. For safety, don't exchange large sums of money all at once if you plan to be in Indonesia for a long time.

Changing Money

Foreign currency, in banknotes and traveller's cheques, is best exchanged at major banks or authorised money-changers. The best rates are in Kuta; Ubud rates are slightly lower. It is pos-

Hours and Holidays
Government offices are open Mon–Thur 8am–3pm, Fri 8am–noon. Banking hours are Mon–Fri from 9am–3pm. Retail shops, especially in tourist areas, are open daily from 9am–9pm, but many in the cities close on Sun.

Maps
Free maps of the island are available at many Balinese travel agencies. Most bookstores also stock maps of Bali. Useful publications are the Periplus Travel Maps of Bali and also of Lombok and Sumbawa. The Periplus Street Atlas Bali is a detailed

Above from left:
temple anniversary
(odilan), Pura Silay-
akti, Padangbai;
Taman Tirtagangga
water park.

**Taxes and
Tipping**
Most hotels and
restaurants add at
least a 10 percent
government tax on
to your bill, with
many high-end
places charging up
to a whopping 21
percent for tax and
service. Tips for
attentive service
are appreciated in
places without a
service charge.
If you hire a car
and like the driver,
then a tip of
10–15 percent
is appreciated.
Always carry small
banknotes with you,
as taxi drivers are
often short of
change, or so they
claim. Rounding up
the fare to the
nearest Rp 10,000
is standard.
An airport or hotel
porter expects at
least Rp 2,000–
5,000 per bag,
depending on its
size and weight.

sible to change money in upmarket hotels but you will find that hotels and airport exchange bureaux generally give rates far below the official exchange rate.

Bring only new and crisp paper currency, especially US dollar bills, as many places will not accept old and faded ones. Smaller US dollar denominations and traveller's cheques usually get a slightly lower exchange rate. Traveller's cheques are accepted at all major hotels and at some shops. Make sure to bring along your passport for identity and signature verification.

If you choose to deal with a money-changer, be extremely careful: they are renowned for their quick fingers and rigged calculators. Beware of ones who offer a higher rate, this is merely a ploy to attract your custom; only use an authorised moneychanger. Make sure you get a receipt for your transaction, and hang on to it. Rupiah may be converted back into foreign currency at the airport when leaving the country. Note that everyone leaving Indonesia from Ngurah Rai International Airport is required to pay an airport tax of Rp 150,000.

Credit Cards

Many large shops accept major credit cards, but an additional 3–5 percent will be added to your bill. Few places outside of the major hotels and big restaurants accept American Express on account of its higher commission charges.

Cash Advances

Cash advances can be obtained in all the major tourist resorts and automatic teller (cash) machines (ATMs) are common now, especially at shopping centres and bank branches.

P

POST

Post offices *(kantor pos)* in major towns open Mon–Thur, 8am–2pm, Fri 8am–noon, Sat 8am–1pm and sometimes (eg in Ubud) Sun 8am–noon. The central post office in Denpasar, Jl Raya Niti Mandala, Renon, is open Mon–Fri 8am–8pm. Post boxes are yellow.

R

RELIGION

Nearly 88 percent of the population in Bali is Hindu; the others are Muslim, Christian and Buddhist. Protestantism is also officially recognised.

T

TELEPHONES

Telephone Area Codes
If calling from within the same region, no area code is needed. If calling from abroad, omit the initial zero.

Note that the country code for Indonesia is **62**.

Area codes are as follows:
- Denpasar, Kuta, Sanur, Nusa Dua, Ubud, Gianyar, Tabanan: 0361
- Singaraja, Lovina, Buleleng: 0362
- Karangasem, Amlapura, Candidasa, Buitan, Amed: 0363
- Negara, Jembrana: 0365
- Bangli, Kintamani, Batur, Klungkung: 0366
- Bedugul, Bratan: 0368
- Lombok: 0370

Mobile (Cell) Phones

Mobile phones, which are known as handphones in Indonesia, can be used in Bali, as long as your phone operates on the GSM network. Alternatively, you can purchase a prepaid phone card and local number for around Rp 50,000. The reception quality for mobiles is generally good.

TOURIST INFORMATION

Denpasar (Ngurah Rai International) Airport: tel: 0361-751011.
Denpasar Government Tourism Office: Jl Surapati 7, Denpasar; tel: 0361-234569.
Badung Tourism Office: Jl S.Parman, Renon; tel: 0361-222387.
Bali Tourism Board: Jl Raya Puputan, Niti Mandala, Denpasar; tel: 0361-239200.
Bali Tourist Information Centre: Jl Bunisari 7, Kuta; tel: 0361-753530.
Bina Wisata Ubud Tourist Office: Jl Raya Ubud; tel: 0361-973285;

8am–8pm.
Buleleng Tourist Office: Jl Veteran 23, Singaraja; tel: 0362-25141; 7.30am–3.30pm.
Jembrana Tourist Office: Jl Dr Setia Budi 1, Negara; tel: 0365-41060.

TRANSPORT

Airport and Arrival

The domestic departures and arrivals terminal is the terminal closest to the main gates of the airport. The international arrivals terminal is in the centre, while the departures terminal is at the far end. All are within a few minutes' walking distance of each other.

Denpasar Airport (also known as Ngurah Rai International Airport): tel: 0361-751025/0361-751011; Customs tel: 0361-756714; http://dps.ngurahrai-airport.co.id. Office hours: Mon–Thur 8am–4.30pm, Fri 8am–3.30pm.

Travelling from the airport, and subject to the flow of the traffic, it will take approximately 15 minutes to reach Kuta, 20–25 minutes to Legian, 30 minutes to Seminyak, 40 minutes to Kerobokan, 45–50 minutes to Canggu, 25 minutes to Sanur, 20 minutes to Nusa Dua, 10 minutes to Jimbaran, 75 minutes to Ubud and three hours to Lovina.

If you have not made prior arrangements with your hotel to pick you up, there is a taxi service from the airport in Bali that you can use; fixed rates to various destinations are posted at the

Time Zones
Bali follows Central Indonesian Standard Time, eight hours ahead of Greenwich Mean Time. It is one hour ahead of Java, and in the same time zone as Singapore.

Toilets
There are few public toilets in Bali, and those that exist are generally dirty and unpleasant. Better maintained public toilets can occasionally be found at the site of tourist attractions, where you will be expected to make a nominal payment of around Rp 500 per visit. Alternatively, if you're prepared to pay for a drink, you will always be able to use the toilet in a restaurant or *warung*. Expect squat toilets and no toilet paper in the simple *warungs*.

Above from left:
fishing boats on
Danau Bratan;
street in Singaraja.

counter. Pay the cashier at the desk and receive a coupon that is to be handed over to your driver, who will be summoned for you.

There are no other forms of public transport from the airport apart from taxis and hotel pick-up services.

Public Transport

Minivans

Minivans *(bemo)* operate on fixed routes from terminals or marketplaces in cities and major towns. Some transfer points are at important crossroads. There are no marked places to get off and on; just flag them down and call out 'stop' when you want to get out. Fares are based on distance travelled and always very cheap, ranging from just Rp 1,000 to a few thousand rupiah. Always carry small change with you; you can't expect a *bemo* driver to give you change from a Rp 50,000, or even a Rp 20,000, banknote.

As passengers and products get loaded off and on, vans can get hot and crowded. This mode of transport does take time but allows you to meet local people; beware of pickpockets, though.

Buses

Major bus terminals are at Tegal in Denpasar (services to Kuta); Kereneng in Denpasar (services to destinations within the city, Batubulan and Sanur); Ubung (services to Tabanan, Singaraja and Jembrana); Batubulan (services to Gianyar, Singaraja, Bangli, Klungkung

and Karangasem) and in Singaraja (services to Jembrana, Tabanan, Denpasar and Karangasem).

Shuttle Services

Shuttle services operate daily between Kuta, Ubud, Sanur, Lovina and Candidasa. Although they cost a bit more than buses or *bemo*, they are faster and more comfortable. Tickets are available from most hotels and tourist agencies.

Taxis

Taxis are metered or have fixed rates from the airport to the major hotels. Check with the driver before you board the taxi, as many drivers prefer to charge a flat rate instead of using the meter. Ask your hotel concierge what the going rate is for the destination you want to get to. Few taxis, outside of the Kuta-Legian-Seminyak area, cruise the streets for passengers, so you need to call up (or ask your hotel concierge to call a taxi for you). The best company is Bali Taxi (Bluebird Group, *see below*), the light blue cabs, with a reputation for being clean, reliable, safe and honest. Most drivers speak English, especially the drivers of Bali Taxi cabs.

Bali Taxi, tel: 0361-701111 (complaints tel: 0361-701621)

There are very few taxis in Ubud; the only ones you will see are those that have brought passengers from other tourist areas and are hoping for a fare back. You can arrange private transport with your hotel or negotiate

Motorcycle Taxis
Young men operate
motorcycle taxis
known as *ojek*,
which can be very
convenient for
locations not
serviced by public
transport. Agree
on the price
beforehand, and
make sure you wear
the extra helmet that
the driver provides,
as it's required by
law. The drivers do
weave in and out of
heavy traffic but are
very experienced.
Fares are usually just
a few thousand
rupiah for a short
journey and no more
than about half of
what you would pay
for a taxi.

a fare with one of the many young men offering transport on the street.

Private Transport
Vehicle with Driver

Chartering a car or minivan with driver can be done by the half-day or full-day. Rates are cheaper if negotiated on the street rather than from your hotel; look out for young men who call out 'transpor' and move their hands as if driving a car. The amount should include fuel. Daily rates are generally between Rp 200,000 and Rp 400,000. Alternatively you can rent a car and pay about Rp 100,000 extra per day for the services of an English-speaking driver.

Motorcycle Hire

Motorcyles are a convenient and inexpensive way to get around the island, but there are risks due to heavy traffic and poor roads. Helmets are required by law, but the cheap ones provided by rental agencies offer little protection, so bring your own or buy a good one from a local shop, especially one with a face shield for protection from sun, rain, bugs and dust. Drive slowly and defensively, as locals and tourists are injured or killed every year in accidents.

The cost of motorbike hire varies according to the model, condition of the machine, length of rental, and time of the year. Around Rp 50,000 to Rp 100,000 per day is usual. Petrol is not included. Buy full insurance so that you are not responsible for any damage. Be sure to test drive your bike, to check that everything is in working order, especially brakes and lights. Most rental bikes are 125cc or smaller.

You should have an international driving permit valid for motorcycles, or else go to the Denpasar Police Office to obtain a temporary permit, valid for three months on Bali only. Normally the person who rents you the motorbike will accompany you to the police office. Bring your passport, driving licence from your home country, and three passport-sized photographs.

V

VISAS AND PASSPORTS

The following information is accurate at time of press, but subject to change at any time.

If you have a British, US, Canadian, Australian or New Zealand passport, you are eligible for visa-on-arrival (VOA) when visiting Bali and Indonesia; this costs US$25 for 30 days. Processing is relatively fast, 3–5 minutes per applicant, and those who cannot pay in US dollars can change money on the spot.

Your passport must be valid for at least six months from the date of entry into Indonesia, and you must have proof of onward passage (either return or through tickets).

Private Car Hire
Driving in Bali can be dangerous. Generally, drivers do not drive defensively, the roads are narrow and poorly maintained, and stray dogs and chickens frequently dart into the road. If you collide with anything, you are responsible for all costs. It's safer to hire a driver while you relax and enjoy the sights. Note that driving is on the left-hand side of the road in Bali.

Weights and Measures
Indonesia uses the metric system. Temperatures are measured in degrees Celsius.

Kuta/Legian

Hard Rock Hotel

Jl Kuta Beach, Kuta; tel: 0361-761869; www.hardrockhotels.net/bali; $$$

Hard Rock Hotel honours five decades of rock culture, its live music venues adorned with priceless rock'n'roll memorabilia. There's an in-house radio station, a rock 'n' roll library, and a recording studio where rising stars can cut their own albums. The huge free-form pool has poolside cabins, together with the man-made 'Sand Island', where there's a night-time concert stage for accomplished bands.

Poppies Cottages I

Gang Poppies I, Kuta; tel: 0361-751059; www.poppies.net; $$

Romantic, traditional-style cottages set in private gardens with lily ponds and waterfalls. Each cottage has a thatched roof and a courtyard bathroom with open-air sunken bathtub. There are two swimming pools with landscaped sunbathing terraces, a garden restaurant, library and games area. Often filled to capacity, so reservations are essential.

Price for a double room (subject to a 10–21 percent tax and service charge):

$$$$	over US$200
$$$	US$120–200
$$	US$60–120
$	below US$60

Un's Hotel

Jl Bene Sari 16, Kuta; tel: 0361-757409; www.unshotel.com; $

If you plan to stay in Kuta, you'll find that the Un's Hotel is perfectly located, just five minutes' stroll from the beach on one side and five minutes' walk from the shops and nightspots of busy Jalan Legian on the other. For a budget hotel, this peaceful oasis is great value; its air-conditioned or fan-cooled rooms are bordered by wide communal balconies and terraces set around a swimming pool in a pretty garden.

Seminyak and Canggu

Hotel Tugu Bali

Batu Bolong, Canggu; tel: 0361-731701; www.tuguhotels.com; $$$$

A living museum of priceless antiques and rare cultural artefacts, this spellbinding boutique hotel and spa is set between rice fields and the quiet rugged beach of Canggu. The property is reminiscent of a village; wooden houses overhang cobbled alleyways bordered by hedges. Two suites contain replica studios of famous painters who discovered Bali in the 1930s; there is an exceptional spa, and the dining facilities include the atmospheric 300-year-old Kang Xi period temple.

The Legian

Jl Kayu Aya, Petitenget; tel: 0361-730622; www.ghmhotels.com; $$$$

This all-suite hotel is set within lovely gardens beside a tranquil stretch of

Above from far left: Hard Rock Hotel; The Legian; Ayana Resort and Spa.

Seminyak Beach. Each spacious suite incorporates private balconies from which to take in the magnificent coastline view. Local craftsmanship is on display within The Legian's peaked roofs and bare wooden columns and rafters, while intricate Indonesian sculptures will greet you in the impressive lobby. There's a fabulous pool here and an excellent restaurant.

The Oberoi

Jl Kayu Aya, Petitenget; tel: 0361-730361; www.oberoihotels.com; $$$$

With a history that spans three decades, The Oberoi truly embraces the culture of the island. The hotel is positioned right beside the beach and comprises Balinese-style cottages and villas set in landscaped gardens. Other nice touches include villa pools, private courtyards and open-air massage parlours, while the main swimming pool is reminiscent of an ancient Balinese bathing place. There are two restaurants, recreational facilities and cultural performances.

Jimbaran Bay

Ayana Resort and Spa

Jl Karang Mas Sejahtera, Jimbaran; tel: 0361-702222; www.ayanaresort. com; $$$

Rebranded from Ritz-Carlton, this exceptional resort occupies a spectacular cliff-top setting. It offers a wide variety of accommodation as well as an almost overwhelming choice of recreational facilities, restaurants, spa venues, swim-

ming pools and wedding venues (including two ultra avant-garde wedding chapels). The modern Balinese architecture is complemented by ornate doors, whimsical stone carvings and Indonesian artwork. Pools and waterfalls cascade towards the ocean, and a series of romantic open pavilions are encompassed by lotus ponds.

Four Seasons Resort

Jl Uluwatu, Jimbaran; tel: 0361-701010; www.fourseasons.com; $$$$

The gorgeous gardens of this luxury villa resort roll down to a beautiful sandy beach. The villas are spacious with thatched roofs, private gardens, plunge pools and secluded open-air bathrooms; the two sumptuous royal villas and nine private residences (with two, three and four bedrooms) all have private swimming pools. Additionally, you'll find five restaurants, a multi-award-winning spa, and the Ganesha Art Gallery. Tennis courts and a cookery school are also on site.

The Bukit

Karma Kandara

Banjar Wijaya Kusuma, Ungasan; tel: 0361-848 2200; www.karmakandara.com; $$$$

Blessed with an intoxicating view of the Indian Ocean, this stunning, five-star resort has everything that you could possibly require within a single package, including luxurious villa accommodation, 24-hour reception, security and

Choosing a Hotel
Bali has a very wide range of accommodation, from over-the-top luxury hotels to cheap family-run guesthouses (also known as *losmen*). Most top-end hotels in Kuta, Jimbaran, Sanur and Nusa Dua are located on the beach and are of international standards.

Peak Periods
Many places have
slightly higher rates
during the peak
tourist season from
July to August, and
from mid-December
to mid-January.
Reservations are
recommended for
the larger hotels
during these peak
periods. In the low
season negotiate
for lower rates.

room service, childcare amenities, a spectacular Balinese spa and a glamorous fine dining restaurant. It even has the facility of a private cliff inclinator, providing access to Karma Kandara's pristine beach, beach club and bar.

Sanur
Bali Hyatt
Jl Bali Hyatt; tel: 0361-288271; www.balihyatt.com; $$$

Bali Hyatt has been flourishing in Sanur for well over three decades, and its facilities are as complete as you will find anywhere in Bali. Accommodation consists of 390 rooms and suites, many with sea views; amenities include restaurants, swimming pools, a children's club, a convention centre and a gorgeous spa set within its own compound. However, it's the botanical gardens that add the real wow factor.

Hotel Sanur Beach
Jl Danau Tamblingan, Semawang; tel: 0361-288011; www.sanur beachhotelbali.com; $$

This long-established hotel, with its four-storey block and exclusive bun-

galows set in landscaped gardens on the beach, is renowned for its friendly staff and excellent service. It offers a range of sports facilities and restaurants that serve Indonesian, Italian, Mexican and South American food.

Nusa Dua/Tanjung Benoa
Conrad Bali
Jl Pratama, Tanjung Benoa; tel: 0361-778788; www.conradhotels. com; $$$

Situated in a prime location on the long finger-shaped cape of Tanjung Benoa, this five-star resort embraces families, honeymooners and business travellers with a wide range of facilities and leisure options. A sparkling lagoon pool, complete with romantic Venetian-style bridges and a sandy-bottomed shallow area for kids, meanders past thatched massage pavilions, guest rooms, bars, restaurants and a 300m/yd crescent of pristine beach.

Grand Hyatt Bali
Nusa Dua; tel: 0361-771234/772038; www.hyatt.com; $$$

Grand Hyatt is the island's largest resort, served by five restaurants, and numerous amenities. Styled after a fabled Balinese water palace, the hotel has an aquatic theme that begins at the lobby then ebbs and flows down to the ocean, transforming en route into lakes, moats, lagoons, rivers, waterfall-fed rock pools and swimming pools, linked by meandering pathways and straddled by

Price for a double room (subject to a 10–21 percent tax and service charge):	
$$$$	over US$200
$$$	US$120–200
$$	US$60–120
$	below US$60

hump-back bridges. The beautiful gardens are bordered by a 650m/yd white-sand beach offering sunbathing, safe swimming and water sports.

Four Seasons Sayan

Sayan, Ubud; tel: 0361-977577; www.fourseasons.com; $$$$

This exclusive resort is situated on the banks of the Ayung River gorge, and the approach is via a solid teak bridge, which leads to an awesome lotus pond, resting on the roof of the main building like a giant flying saucer hovering above the trees. The vista of the river as it coils its way through the chasm below is spectacular. Accommodation here comprises 60 units; 42 of these are villas and the remaining 18 are suites. A treatment in the riverside spa is an experience that you will never forget.

Tegal Sari

Jl Hanoman, Padang Tegal, Ubud; tel: 0361-975376; www.tegalsari-ubud.com; $

This romantic hotel rests within an enviable, peaceful location in the middle of the rice fields, just 1½km (1 mile) from the centre of Ubud. It offers the choice of rooms and duplex bungalows, each one different. There is also a swimming pool, a massage pavilion, an open-air fitness arena, dining *bales*, lotus ponds and a restaurant. This is probably the best-value budget hotel in Ubud and popular, so book well in advance.

Ubud Hanging Gardens

Desa Buahan, Desa Payangan; tel: 0361-982700; www.ubud hanginggardens.com; $$$$

Steeply set amid the rice terraces of Ubud are 38 private villas, each with its own infinity plunge pool and spa. The resort's Beduur restaurant, which serves wonderful French-Asian haute cuisine, is accessed by a private funicular. It clings to the side of a river gorge with views of a floodlit temple, which at night appears to be magically floating upon the clouds.

Ulun Ubud

Sanggingan, Ubud; tel: 0361-975024; www.ulunubud.com; $$

A gem of a hotel carved into the hillside, this delightful place offers excellent value for money with spacious cottages, a restaurant and a spring-fed infinity pool presenting stunning views of the Campuhan River, the jungle and paddy fields. The hotel was created by a Balinese family of artists, so there are some beautiful artworks here.

Lakeview Restaurant & Hotel

Penelokan, Kintamani; tel: 0366-51394; www.indo.com/hotels/lakeview; $

Perched on the rim of the ancient caldera, this place offers 14 spacious rooms, each with views of the volcano and lake from both the bed and the bathroom. You can watch the sunrise over the lake

Above from far left: breakfast at the Conrad Bali; wonderfully tranquil pool; the Four Seasons Sayan.

What to Expect
Deluxe and luxury accommodation will include hot water, air conditioning, and usually IDD telephone and other facilities. Budget and economy places often include a simple breakfast.

from your balcony, or sit out at night under the stars, enjoying the twinkling lights from the eight fishing villages known as *bintang danu* (stars of the lake) dotted around the water's edge.

Candidasa

Alila Manggis

Buitan, Manggis; tel: 0363-41011; www.alilahotels.com/Manggis; $$$$

This Green Globe-certified boutique resort in the peaceful beachside village of Manggis has won numerous awards for its commitment to responsible tourism. There's an organic garden, and the spa products are all-natural. The suites, rooms, restaurant, spa and swimming pool are set within a coconut grove garden that gently rolls on to Buitan Beach. The hotel is famous for its cookery school, which teaches how to prepare Balinese cuisine.

Amankila Resort

Manggis, Karangasem; tel: 0363-41333; www.amankila.com; $$$$

The ultraluxe Amankila Resort is comprised of a cluster of thatched pavilions, two restaurants, a private beach club

and a spectacular three-tiered swimming pool, cascading downhill to shimmering Labuanamuk Bay – the vista is eye-boggling. The stand-alone suites rest on stilts, maximising the views; each features a shaded outdoor terrace, while nine enjoy private pools.

Amarta

Candidasa; tel: 0363-41230; $

If you're looking for budget accommodation, you can't go wrong with Amarta. These Western-owned beachside bungalows are excellent value for money and a favourite with Bali's expats. The staff are friendly, and the restaurant serves wholesome food and seriously good hearty breakfasts included in the room rate. Simple and rustic accommodation comes with a choice of either air-conditioned or fan-cooled rooms.

Nusa Lembongan

Hai Tide Huts

Mushroom Bay, Nusa Lembongan; tel: 0366-720331; www.balihai cruises.com/html/index.php?id=4; $$

Each of these romantic, rice-barn-style thatch and bamboo huts has a bedroom accessed by a ladder. Stylish and immaculate furnishings, combined with air conditioning and room service, transform this traditionally simple accommodation into something that is ethnic chic. The colourful bathrooms are shared and located a few metres from the huts. Facilities include a swimming pool, restaurant, and beach club.

Price for a double room (subject to a 10–21 percent tax and service charge):	
$$$$	over US$200
$$$	US$120–200
$$	US$60–120
$	below US$60

Adirama

Jl Raya Lovina; tel: 0362-41759;
www.adiramabeachhotel.com; $
This old beach-front hotel is Dutch-owned and excellent value for money. Recently renovated with attractive new furnishings and new bathrooms, each room has a private balcony overlooking the swimming pool. There is a small spa and an attractive sea-front restaurant.

Damai Lovina Villas

Jl Damai, Kayuputih, Lovina; tel:
0362-41008; www.damai.com; $$$
Intimate retreat a short distance inland from Bali's north coast. It has just eight luxurious villa-style rooms, with four-poster beds, hand-carved doors and en suite bathrooms with jacuzzi tubs under the stars. The setting is a hidden paradise, with cascading gardens and an azure sea shimmering in the distance. The resort harvests its own rice and organic produce, which is then served in its renowned gourmet restaurant.

Bedugul

Pacung Mountain Resort

Jl Raya Pacung, Baturiti; tel: 0368-21038/9; www.balileisure.com/h/pacung-resort/index.html; $$$
This hillside resort is the only hotel in the area with a swimming pool; it also has a beautiful vista of the valley and Gunung Batukau. Accommodation is comprised of rooms, or attractive thatched cottages with balconies and rice-field views. A gondola transports guests from their rooms to the pool. There is also a restaurant, but no air conditioning in this cool climate.

Tabanan

Gajah Mina Beach Resort

Suraberata, Lalanglinggah,
Selemadeg, Tabanan;
mobile: 081-934-355633;
www.gajahminaresort.com; $$
This charming hotel offers individual Balinese-style villas, a restaurant and a swimming pool, all spread across a dazzling headland surmounting a private beach. The restaurant is a delight, utilising fresh produce from the hotel's own garden. Remote, but an ideal choice for those looking to escape the hustle and bustle of the tourist areas.

Taro

Elephant Safari Park Lodge

Jalan Elephant Park, Taro,
Tegallalang; tel: 0361-721480;
www.elephantsafariparklodge.com;
$$$$
Pack a trunk and stay over for a night or two in the luxurious safari-style lodge of the Elephant Safari Park, with its swimming pool, bar, lounge, gym, spa and four different styles of air-conditioned accommodation, with big windows and terraces for elephant watching. Elegant interiors are set off by custom-made, elephant-themed accessories, such as bed legs crafted in the form of elephant feet.

Above from far left: Ayana Resort and Spa *(see p.95)*; looking out from the Lakeview *(see p.97)*; star treatment by the pool.

Villas and Apartments
Other options to staying in a hotel include renting fully serviced apartments, and, if there are a few of you, you may elect to hire a villa with its own staff; Elite Havens (www.EliteHavens.com), a villa-management agency based in Bali, has a sterling reputation. You can also choose to stay in a private villa-style hotel, set within a secure complex.

New restaurants open and close all the time in Bali. The following selection includes tried-and-tested establishments, plus new finds; this is just the tip of the iceberg, of course. Many hotels also have restaurants serving good food. In the tourist centres of Sanur, Kuta/Legian and Nusa Dua, restaurants usually serve lunch from 11am–3pm, and dinner (some with dance performances) from 6–10pm daily. Seminyak has the highest concentration of independent fine-dining restaurants on the island. A number of restaurants open all day, including for breakfast. In Ubud, Lovina and Candidasa, restaurants open from 11am–9pm daily.

Sanur

Café Batujimbar

Jl Danau Tamblingan 75, Sanur; tel: 0361-287374; $$

This is a popular street-side café and long-time favourite of people who know Sanur. Dining takes place in an open-sided pavilion or alfresco under the trees. Italian and Mexican dishes grace the menu, including pastas and quesadillas, together with healthy salads, home-made breads and cakes, herbal teas and booster fruit juices. Organic vegetables and herbs are grown at the owner's farm near Bedugul.

Jazz Bar & Grille

Komplex Pertokoan Sanur Raya 15–16, Jl Bypass Ngurah Rai, Sanur; tel: 0361-285892; $$

This long-established restaurant offers everything from sandwiches, snacks and pizzas, to four-course meals. Plenty of cosy alcoves, a regular line-up of live music acts and a large menu presenting classic Western and Indonesian dishes – including Jazz Grille nachos, *sop buntut*, *gado gado* and wonderful puddings.

Massimo il Ristorante

Jl Danau Tamblingan 206, Sanur; tel: 0361-288942; $$

This is a great Italian restaurant, set in an attractive open pavilion surrounded by a garden. The menu offers authentic specialities from Lecce in southeast Italy, where the owner-chef Massimo hails from. The pasta dishes and thin-crust wood-fired oven pizzas are all good. Massimo also does an excellent risotto with mushrooms and Italian sausage, as well as beef fillets, chicken, duck and fish specialities, and the best Italian ice cream in Bali.

Mezzanine Restaurant & Bar

Jl Danau Tamblingan 63, Sanur; tel: 0361-270624; $$$

A stylish restaurant with helpful and friendly staff and an interesting blend of Thai, Japanese, Chinese and Western dishes on the menu. The colonial-style building, vast, open-sided and broad-pillared, features a varied choice of dining areas – from breezy terrace at

the front to cosy mezzanine. The menu lists well over 100 items, a Teppanyaki Grill and seafood from the large fish tank among them.

Sanur Beach Market
Jl Segara Ayu on the beach; tel: 0361-289374; $

This beach-side restaurant is excellent for grilled seafood and dessert. Choose the dance performance and special set dinner on one day a week, or order from the menu without cover charge.

Stiff Chilli
Jl Kesumasari 11, Semawang; tel: 0361-288371; $$

A rustic open-sided pavilion beside the beach, serving Italian cuisine with an Asian twist. This highly respected restaurant is famous for its crispy-skinned, grilled sausages, freshly baked ciabatta bread, authentic Italian pizzas and pasta delights, such as the tri-coloured fettuccine topped with creamy smoked marlin sauce.

Kuta/Legian

For inexpensive and delicious grilled seafood at night, head for the Kuta Night Market. The food is very easy on the pocket just as long as you avoid going for the lobster.

Aromas Restaurant
Jl Legian; tel: 0361-751003; $$

This entirely vegetarian restaurant uses no eggs. The huge menu offers local and international vegetarian dishes, salads and dips, from India, Thailand, the Middle East, Mexico and Europe. A large open-air pavilion provides the setting, surrounded by shrubs, water and fountains, and offering a pleasant retreat from the hustle and bustle of Jalan Legian itself.

Kori Restaurant & Bar
Jl Gang Poppies II, Kuta; tel: 0361-758605; $$$

Escape from the Kuta crowds to this quiet retreat with wonderful Balinese ambience and a lotus pond nearby; pick from low-cushioned seating or colonial-style chairs and marble-topped tables. The international menu offers delicious fresh seafood, imported steaks, favourites such as char-grilled bangers and mash, and warm sticky-toffee date pudding topped with butterscotch sauce.

Made's Warung
Jl Pantai Kuta; tel: 0361-755297; $$

One of the first places to cater for foreigners when it was one of only two eateries on Kuta's main street, and

Above from far left: Gianyar food market; Kori Restaurant & Bar.

Price for a two-course meal for one including a non-alcoholic beverage:

$$$$	over Rp 300,000
$$$	Rp 200,000–300,000
$$	Rp 100,000–200,000
$	below Rp 100,000

still popular for its menu of local and international dishes and delicious desserts. A second branch, Made's Warung II (tel: 0361-732130) is located in Seminyak.

Poppies Restaurant
Gang Poppies I, Kuta; tel: 0361-751059; $$$

Poppies Restaurant has been serving punters since 1973 and enjoys a romantic garden setting, amid pools and fountains sheltered by pergolas draped in cascading thunbergia. Open for breakfast, lunch and dinner, with free WiFi from 8am until 7pm, Poppies offers a good selection of Asian and Western dishes including fresh fish and seafood, home-made soups, salads, pasta dishes and steaks. There are plenty of classic Indonesian specialities, while vegetarians are also well looked after.

TJ's Mexican Restaurant
Gang Poppies I; tel: 0361-751093; $$

This popular restaurant is known for its colourful decor and garden setting. The menu offers superb, authentic Californian-Mexican cuisine with delicious starters and the best loaded nachos, buffalo wings, quesadilla, tacos, enchiladas, tostadas, fajitas and margaritas this side of the Pacific. Try the aubergine or tofu and bean dip with chips and finish with the mango cheesecake with raspberry sauce.

Seminyak
Gateway of India
Jl Abimanyu, Seminyak; tel: 0361-732940; $

With an Indian owner married to a Balinese, you can be assured of authentic Indian fare. The tandoori dishes and the freshly baked naan breads are wonderful, and be sure to try the lamb or chicken *kathi* roll, a sort of pancake bursting with a spicy filling. Very casual, so dress down for dinner. There are also branches in Sanur (tel: 0361-281579) and Kuta (tel: 0361-754463).

The Junction
Jl Laksmana/Kayu Aya, Seminyak; tel: 0361-735610; $$

The Junction has fresh green-and-white decor with a variety of seating areas, including a lounge and a colonial-style verandah. They specialise in organic salads made with gourmet ingredients and also do sassy sandwiches in the form of panini, pitta pockets, crêpes and baguettes. There are top-quality mains, too, if you fancy something more substantial.

Price for a two-course meal for one including a non-alcoholic beverage:

$$$$	over Rp 300,000
$$$	Rp 200,000–300,000
$$	Rp 100,000–200,000
$	below Rp 100,000

Ku De Ta

Jl Laksmana, Petitenget; tel: 0361–736969 ; $$$$

Bali's famous restaurant, beach club and sophisticated hotspot is the place to see and be seen, especially at sunset, when the setting is spectacular. Ku De Ta offers hearty breakfasts, excellent lunches and intimate dining at night, with a classy menu of contemporary Australian cuisine.

La Lucciola Restaurant & Bar

Jl Kayu Aya, Petitenget; tel: 0361-261047; $$$

Delicious Mediterranean and Italian food and a casual atmosphere are the hallmarks of this big, two-level thatched structure, which looks out over the beach. It's great for sunset cocktails and is usually packed for dinner. Reservations are essential, otherwise expect to wait at least an hour for a table.

Métis

Jl Petitenget 6; tel: 0361-737888; $$$$

From the owners of the former and fabulous Kafé Warisan, this large and sophisticated fine dining restaurant, bar, lounge and gallery beside the rice fields serves French-Mediterranean cuisine. The menu includes the famous pan-seared hot foie gras with port and raspberry reduction, morelo cherry and roasted apple.

Sardine

Jl Petitenget; tel: 0361-738202; $$$$

The extraordinary Sardine features a polished bamboo bar and a gourmet menu, where the emphasis is on fresh fish and seafood – meat and vegetarian dishes do get a look in too. The restaurant overlooks a working rice field, which the owners have purchased in order to protect their views and then embellished with special lighting, coloured flags and giant urns.

Trattoria

Jl Laksmana/Kayu Aya; tel: 0361-737082; $$

Packed almost every night of the week, which says a lot about the food (and the reasonable prices) here. There are fantastic pastas, pizzas and salads as well as beef and seafood dishes, but be prepared to wait if you don't have a reservation. Tables are packed tightly together in this smallish restaurant with a lively atmosphere.

Nusa Dua/Tanjung Benoa

Bumbu Bali

Jl Pratama, Tanjung Benoa; tel: 0361-774502; $$$

'Bumbu' means spice paste, and this restaurant is renowned for its long menu of authentic, beautifully presented Balinese dishes – seafood and duck in banana leaf lead the specialities. You can also sign up for cookery classes, and free transport to Bumbu

Above from far left: Poppies Restaurant; showcasing the art of presentation.

Bali is provided by hotels in the area. Traditional Balinese dance shows on some nights.

Nampu
Grand Hyatt, Nusa Dua; tel: 0361-771234; $$$$

A superb Japanese fine-dining restaurant with a choice of eating experiences including a Teppanyaki room, private Tatami rooms and a sophisticated dining room. Serves beautifully presented, high-quality sashimi, sushi, tempura, charcoal-grilled dishes and much more.

Jimbaran Bay

Try the grilled seafood places that open around sunset along the beach. Lots of smoke, but the food is tasty and the setting pleasant. Particularly good is **Ayu Wandira** (tel: 0361-701950), which dishes up a huge barbecued seafood platter. $$

Denpasar

Danau Toba
Jl Teuku Umar 74X; tel: 0361-263553; $$

Danau Toba is named after a famous lake in Sumatra, and the Chinese-Indonesian food served here comes from Medan in the same area. The menu offers a choice of small, medium, or large portions of fish, lobster, crab, prawn, squid, pigeon, duck, chicken, tofu, beef, frog and vegetables in a wide selection of different sauces. The rather gaudy Chinese decor features lucky mobiles and kitsch artwork, spinning circular tables facilitate the sharing of dishes, and tanks of live fish promise some super-fresh dishes.

Rasa Sayang
Jl Teuku Umar, Denpasar; tel: 0361-262006; $$

Local people claim that this Chinese restaurant is one of the best in Denpasar. The interior is simple, the decor is plain, and although the supermarket-style piped music doesn't do much for the ambience, the delicious food compensates for the lack of atmosphere. Delicacies include fish-head soup, lettuce buns, raw lobster with wasabi, deep-fried squid in Worcester sauce and sliced beef with Chinese broccoli.

Sunda Kelapa
Jl Teuku Umar 183, Denpasar; tel: 0361-233481; $

In common with most *warungs* (simple restaurants) in Denpasar, Sunda Kelapa is where the locals eat. The food is authentic Jakartan cuisine and includes dishes such as traditional style *gado gado* (Javanese vegetable salad served with peanut sauce), *tempe penyet* (fermented soya-bean cake, crushed), *bakso kuah* (beef meatballs in gravy), frogs' legs, *rujak manis* (a raw vegetable and fruit salad in a hot and spicy tamarind dressing), marrow bone soup and *mie* (noodles fried in coconut oil) with fish, squid or chicken.

Ubud

Bebek Bengil (Dirty Duck)

Jl Hanuman, Padangtegal; tel: 0361-975489 $$

An Ubud institution, this sprawling open-air garden restaurant and bar is surrounded by rice fields with numerous cosy and intimate spots for eating and drinking. It promotes popular local dishes and European-style home cooking, with an extensive menu that includes Bali's famous crispy duck, as well as bratwurst and mash, *nasi campur*, imported steaks and old-fashioned apple crumble.

Casa Luna

Jl Raya Ubud; tel: 0361-973283; $$

This semi open-air, café-style restaurant on different levels has a laid-back vibe and is renowned for its Sunday brunch, breakfast and cakes. The menu options are international and Indonesian specialities, including vegetarian spring rolls, smoked marlin salad, spiced coconut fish and delectable offerings from the Honeymoon Bakery.

Price for a two-course meal for one including a non-alcoholic beverage:

$$$$	over Rp 300,000
$$$	Rp 200,000–300,000
$$	Rp 100,000–200,000
$	below Rp 100,000

Tut Mak

Jl Dewi Sita; tel: 0361-975754; $$

This friendly, café-style restaurant offers a variety of eating areas and is popular with expats. It serves great breakfasts and its omelettes are a highlight, but sandwiches, burgers, dips, snacks and full meals, including Indonesian specialities, all put in an appearance too. There is also a children's menu.

Lovina/Buleleng

Khi Khi Seafood Restaurant

Kalibukbuk, Lovina; tel: 0362-41548; $

An old favourite, this long-established, large seafood restaurant is very popular with the locals. Serves Indonesian and Japanese cuisine – including sushi, *mie goreng* and *nasi goreng* – grilled fresh fish, prawns, calamari and a variety of Chinese specialities such as *cap cay* and sweet and sour dishes.

Candidasa/Karangasem

Garpu

Jl Raya Sengkidu, Candidasa; tel: 0363-49174; $$

This quality restaurant is situated right beside the sea, with a lounge and a poolside area. Garpu means 'fork' in Indonesian, and this theme is reflected in the stylish architecture and interior design. The *à la carte*, *table d'hôte* and buffet menus showcase specialities from the Mediterranean (especially France and Italy) and Bali.

Above from far left: a food cart plies its wares, Gianyar; *bebek betutu* (steamed duck) and various accompaniments.

There is no shortage of nightclubs, dance-bars, discos and bars with live music in Bali's tourist areas. Kuta tends to start throbbing earlier than Seminyak and closes earlier, at around 3 or 4am. The dance-bars in Seminyak usually start getting busy at around 11pm; at some of these, you can party until sunrise, but don't expect them to start pumping until about 2am.

The bars in Sanur generally close at midnight. Here, the scene is more relaxed and mellow, with a few low-key dance clubs that attract a more mature crowd. Older Indonesian businessmen often frequent them, more as a place to relax than for the dancing.

There's not much nightlife in Ubud, and the majority of venues here are closed before midnight. Nusa Dua is not an area known for its nightlife scene, although every hotel has its own bars and sometimes a nightclub. Gambling is illegal in Indonesia, so there are no casinos around.

Below are listed the most popular venues, some of them full-service restaurants with bars that also happen to feature live music.

Kuta/Legian

Centerstage
Hard Rock Hotel, Jl Pantai, Kuta; tel: 0361-5761869
A refined and hi-tech venue dominated by an enormous 5m (16ft) video screen and a plethora of rock memorabilia. Presents live music and entertainment every night from 8.30pm until 11.30pm: slick local bands sing popular covers from a raised stage positioned inside and above the circular central bar, surrounded by video screens and sophisticated lighting. Centerstage doesn't impose a cover charge, but expect to pay upmarket hotel prices for your drinks.

M-Bar-Go
Jl Legian; tel: 0361-756280
M-Bar-Go is a gargantuan nightclub covering two floors with an urban-chic industrial theme, minimal lighting, dark decor and an underground vibe. Glass doors at the front open into a vast, air-conditioned interior space, where resident and guest DJs play booming house music attracting a mixed crowd of surfers, tourists and locals.

Ocean Beach Club
Jl Pantai, Kuta; no tel.
Kuta's biggest and funkiest beach venue comprises a restaurant and grill, sports lounge, swimming pool, bar and nightclub. Nightly dinner shows feature acrobats, fire dancers and show girls.

Seminyak

Bacio
Jl Double Six; tel: 0361-756666

An expansive beach-front nightclub on two levels with a terrace and a large central bar. Here, you can enjoy cool surroundings, smooth vibes and great parties with sounds mixed by resident and guest DJs.

Double Six

Seminyak Beach; tel: 0361-753666

Bali's famous nightclub beside the beach, with international and local DJs playing rousing house and trance music. Busiest at weekends, the club gets going at around 2am and pulsates until dawn. It has several bars, and an air-conditioned interior with large dance floor, outdoor decks and seating around the swimming pool; you can even bungy jump during club hours. Cover charge includes one free drink.

Mannekepis

Jl Raya Seminyak; tel: 0361-8475784

A jazz and blues venue and Belgian bistro rolled into one, Mannekepis has a beautifully styled interior featuring a long bar. Live jazz, blues and rock are performed here on Wednesday, Thursday, Friday and Saturday nights. Upstairs is another large dining area, which spills onto an open-air terrace, complemented by a pool table and table football.

Mixwell

Jl Abimanyu (Dhyana Pura) No. 6, Seminyak; tel: 0361-736864

This popular gay venue is a small lounge bar with an outside terrace. It features DJ music, comedy drag shows and lip-synching divas.

Sanur

Jazz Bar and Grille

Komplek Sanur Raya, J. Bypass Ngurah Rai; tel: 0361-285892

Regular live entertainment performed by well-respected jazz bands from Bali and beyond. The atmosphere is comfortable and cultured, and there is capacity for about 140 people over the two levels.

Ubud

Jazz Café

Jl Sukma; tel: 0361-976594

Opened in 1996 by Balinese Jazz musician Agung Wiryawan, this venue is popular with locals, expats and tourists. There's a friendly atmosphere, superb food, innovative cocktails and exciting live acoustic jazz and ethnic rhythm and blues music performed by local musicians. Closed Mondays.

Ozigo

Jl Sanggingan; tel: 0361-081 2367 9736

Ubud's only nightclub, offering live music at weekends, a dance floor, long curving bar, open-air terrace, and an intimate VIP lounge upstairs. Free transport service offered within the Ubud area.

Above from far left: Ku De Ta (see p.103), a restaurant, beach club and chic hotspot; preparing cocktails.

CREDITS

Insight Step by Step Bali
Written by: Rachel Lovelock
Series Editor: Clare Peel
Editor: Alexia Georgiou
Map Production: original cartography by Berndtson & Berndtson; revised by Stephen Ramsay
Picture Manager: Steven Lawrence
Art Editors: Richard Cooke and Ian Spick
Photography: all pictures Corrie Wingate/APA except 64–5 Jack Hollingsworth/APA; 13, 20B, 58TL Martin Westlake/APA; 4MB Meindert Arnold Jacob/Flickr; 7BR, 98–9 William Cho/Flickr; 21 Curtis Foreman/Flickr; 26–7 Kok Leng Yeo/Flickr; 26BM Danumurthi Mahendra/Flickr; 42–3 AWL Images; 51 Alexis Lê-Quôc/Flickr; 52B, 52M Abdes Prestaka/Flickr; 54TL Karsten Abmann/Flickr; 55TR Jack Merridew/Wikipedia; 56 Zenubud/Flickr; 56TR Alex Smith/Flickr; 58–9 Esme Vos/Flickr; 58B Vosco/Flickr; 62, 102 Chee Hong/Flickr; 67M Dominic Alves/Flickr; 70 Tips Images; 95–6 Peter & Laila/Flickr; 95TL Ronnie Liew/Flickr; 95TR, 98TL Valerio Vao/Flickr; 96TL Tatsuhiko Miyagawa/Flickr; 97TR Mark Lehmkuhler/Flickr; 101 Roger Price/Flickr.
Front cover: Photolibrary, Getty and iStock.
Printed by: CTPS-China

First Edition 2011

CONTACTING THE EDITORS

We would appreciate it if readers would alert us to errors or outdated information by writing to us at insight@apaguide.co.uk or APA Publications, PO Box 7910, London SE1 1WE, UK.

www.insightguides.com

DISTRIBUTION

Worldwide
APA Publications GmbH & Co. Verlag KG (Singapore branch)
7030 Ang Mo Kio Ave 5
08-65 Northstar @ AMK
Singapore 569880
Tel: (65) 570 1051
E-mail: apasin@singnet.com.sg

UK and Ireland
GeoCenter International Ltd
Meridian House, Churchill Way West
Basingstoke, Hampshire, RG21 6YR
Tel: (44) 01256 817 987
E-mail: sales@geocenter.co.uk

US
Langenscheidt Publishers, Inc.
36–36 33rd Street, 4th Floor
Long Island City, NY 11106
Tel: (1) 718 784 0055
E-mail: orders@langenscheidt.com

Australia
Universal Publishers
1 Waterloo Road, Macquarie Park, NSW 2113
Tel: (61) 2 9857 3700
E-mail: sales@universalpublishers.com.au

New Zealand
Hema Maps New Zealand Ltd (HNZ)
Unit 2, 10 Cryers Road
East Tamaki, Auckland 2013
Tel: (64) 9 273 6459
E-mail: sales.hema@clear.net.nz

INDEX